Book of Happiness

Compiled by

Jagdish Gupta

Ocean Books Pvt. Ltd.
ISO 9001:2015 Publishers

Published by
Ocean Books (P) Ltd.
4/19 Asaf Ali Road,
New Delhi-110 002 (INDIA)
e-mail: info@oceanbooks.in

ISBN 978-81-8430-216-5
BOOK OF HAPPINESS
Compiled by Jagdish Gupta

Edition
2025

Price
₹ 500.00 (Rupees Five Hundred only)

Printed at
Narula Printers, Delhi

This book is dedicated to

Charlie Chaplin

the 'Lovable Tramp' of films

who still brings a smile

with his antics.

Contents

A

Abundance: No one wants to take from me what I give abundantly.

—Shirdi Sai Baba

~***~

Abuse: If you cannot endure abuse from another, just say a simple word or two, or else leave.

—Shirdi Sai Baba

~***~

Abuse: The best way of losing a cause is to abuse your opponent and to trade upon his weakness.

—Mahatma Gandhi

~***~

Acceptance: I am willing to accept what I can't change.

—A.P.J. Abdul Kalam

~***~

Accomplishments: Some men dream of worthy accomplishments, while others stay awake and do them.

—Dr. S. Radhakrishnan

~***~

Ache: The only ache people have nowadays is ache in the stomach due to overeating and lack of exercise!

—Sathya Sai Baba

~***~

Acquiring Siddhis: I am opposed to the acquiring of

siddhis (or spiritual attainments); these were obstructions to authentic sadhana.

—Sant Tukaram

~ * * * ~

Act: Learn to speak what you feel, and act what you speak.

—Sathya Sai Baba

~ * * * ~

Act: Thou hast power only to act not over the result thereof. Act thou, therefore, without prospect of the result and without succumbing to inaction.

—Bhagvad Gita

~ * * * ~

Act of charity: A Muslim, who plants a tree or sows a field, from which man, birds and animals can eat, is committing an act of charity.

—Hazrat Muhammad

~ * * * ~

Action and change: Change is crucial. It brings about new thought; new thought leads to innovative action.

—A.P.J. Abdul Kalam

~ * * * ~

Action, love, service: Love cannot remain by itself — it has no meaning. Love has to be put into action, and that action is service.

—Mother Teresa

~ * * * ~

Action, right: It is love alone that leads to right action. What brings order in the world is to love and let love do what it will.

—J. Krishnamurthy

~ * * * ~

Actively engaged: In the present circumstances, no one can afford to assume that someone else will solve their problems. Every individual has a responsibility to help guide our global family in the right direction. Good wishes are not sufficient; we must become actively engaged.

—Dalai Lama

~***~

Acts: Of all the righteous acts, help rendered to those needing it, is the most righteous.

—Sathya Sai Baba

~***~

Administration: You assist an administration most effectively by obeying its orders and decrees. An evil administration never deserves such allegiance.

—Mahatma Gandhi

~***~

Affection: From affection arises grief; from affection arises fear. There is no grief for the one who is free from affection. Whence, then, can there come fear?

—Dhammapada

~***~

Affection: Affection is responsible for nine-tenths of whatever solid and durable happiness there is in our lives.

—C.S. Lewis

~***~

Age and wisdom: So teach us to number our days, that we may apply our hearts unto wisdom.

—Psalms (ch. XC, v. 12)

~***~

Aggrandisement: The man who aims at his own aggrandisement underrates everything else.

—Rabindranath Tagore

~***~

Aggressor: The aggressor always had a purpose behind his attack; he wanted something to be done, some object to be surrendered by the defender.

—Mahatma Gandhi

~***~

Ahimsa: *Ahimsa* is one of the world's greatest principles, which no power on earth can wipe out.

—Mahatma Gandhi

~***~

Aim of our education: I will suggest that the great aim of our education is to bring out of the child, who comes into our hands, every faculty that he brings with him, and then to try to win that child to turn all his abilities, his powers, his capacities, to the helping and serving of the community which is a part.

—Annie Besant

~***~

Ajapa: *Ajapa* (A + Japa = No + Chant) is the primal *Mantra.* This chantless *Mantra* pervades the breath going in and out, the subtle sound 'sah' going in and the subtle sound 'ham' going out.

—Tirumantiram

~***~

All is His: Always bear this in mind: Everything is in God's hands, and you are His tool to be used by Him as He pleases. Try to grasp the significance of 'All is His' and you will immediately feel free from all burdens. What will be the result of your surrender to Him? None will seem alien; all will be your very own Self.

—Anandamayi

~***~

All pervasive: You are the supreme Brahman, infinite, yet hidden in the hearts of all creatures. You pervade everything.

– Svetasvatara Upanishad

~***~

"A": A" is the first and source of all the letters. Even so is God Primordial the first and source of all the world.

—Thirukkural

~***~

Attach and detach: Because you are not concentrated on it. Learn to attach your mind completely to your work while you are doing it, and you will find joy in it.

—Swami Prabhavananda

~***~

All the same: Human beings by nature want happiness and do not want suffering. With that feeling, everyone tries to achieve happiness and tries to get rid of suffering, and everyone has the basic right to do this. In this way, all here are the same, whether rich or poor, educated or uneducated, Easterner or Westerner, believer or non-believer, and within believers whether Buddhist, Christian, Jewish, Muslim, and so on. Basically, from the viewpoint of real human value, we are all the same.

—Dalai Lama

~***~

Allah: Allah is with those who restrain themselves.

—Quran, 16.128

~***~

Alone: A man is born alone and dies alone; and he experiences the good and bad consequences of his *karma* alone; and he goes alone to hell or the Supreme abode.

—Chanakya

~***~

Aloneness and isolation: Loneliness, with its fear and ache, is isolation, the inevitable action of the self. This process of isolation, whether expansive or narrow, is productive of confusion, conflict and sorrow. Isolation can never give birth to aloneness; the one has to cease for the other to be. Aloneness is indivisible and loneliness is separation. That which is alone is pliable and so enduring. Only the alone can commune with that which is causeless, the immeasurable. To the alone, life is eternal; to the alone, there is no death. The alone can never cease to be.

— J. Krishnamurthy

~***~

Angel: I have been transformed from a mortal being

into an angel, in an instant; the True Guru has taught me this. Born of human flesh, I have conquered the heavens; such is the medicine I was given.

—Sant Namdev

~***~

Angels: Hard work and perseverance are beautiful angels, who will reside on your shoulders.

—A.P.J. Abdul Kalam

~***~

Anger: I do not want to foresee the future. I am concerned with taking care of the present. God has given me no control over the moment following.

—Mahatma Gandhi

~***~

Action: Action expresses priorities.

—Mahatma Gandhi

~***~

Anger: I get angry with none.
Will a mother get angry with her children?
Will the ocean send back the waters to the several rivers?

—Shirdi Sai Baba

~***~

Anger: Regretting, regretting, regretting—every minute you are regretting, and so you are angry. You know how anger comes? It piles up. Drop by drop, it collects.

—Sri Sri Ravishankar

~***~

Another man's guilt: The mind is everything. It is in the mind alone that one feels pure and impure. A man, first of all must make his own mind guilty and then alone can he see another man's guilt.

—Sarada Devi

~***~

Another's: Always respect another's opinion and another's point of view.

—Sathya Sai Baba

~***~

Answer, desire: Freedom from the desire for an answer is essential to the understanding of a problem.

—J. Krishnamurthy

~***~

Appointment with future: Disappointment can come only to those Who make an Appointment with the future.

—Swami Chinmayananda

~***~

Arguing mind: Look at this arguing mind. This is what you have been carrying all these years and you want to continue carrying it.

—Sri Sri Ravishankar

~***~

Arjuna defined: Arjuna depicts our physical body and our ego. The five horses drawing the chariot are one's five senses...sight, smell, hearing, touch and taste. Without Krishna, the charioteer, the horses would've simply taken Arjuna anywhere and everywhere. Krishna depicts many things to many people—God, instincts, heart, conscience—basically some inner voice within us that is beyond our intellect. The enemies—the Kouravas—are not external enemies, they are the enemies within the person—like anger, greed and all that kind of thing—and these are the enemies that a person, rather than run away, must face and conquer.

—Osho

~***~

Arrival, departure: They arrive and others arrive. And then they go, and others go. Day and night, a constant traffic. Where do they come from? Where do they go? Does it mean anything? Nothing. Nothing.

—Lal Ded

~***~

Art: What is Art? It is the response of man's creative soul to the call of the real.

—Rabindranath Tagore

~***~

Art: The truth of art is not in substance or logic, but in expression. Abstract truth may belong to science and metaphysics, but the world of reality belongs to art.

—Rabindranath Tagore

~***~

Ask, seek, knock: Ask, and it shall be given to you; seek, and you shall find; knock, and it shall be opened unto you. For everyone that asketh receiveth; and he that seeketh findeth; and to him that knocketh, it shall be opened.

—Matthew 7:7-8

~***~

Asoka's wheel: Asoka's wheel represents to us the wheel of law, the wheel of *Dharm*.. the wheel indicates to us that there is death in stagnation, there is life in movement.

—Dr. S. Radhakrishnan

~***~

Asset: The precious asset of a country is the skill, ingenuity and imagination of its people.

—A.P.J. Abdul Kalam

~***~

Assimilation: The assimilation of the Mahomedan culture also was done in the mind to a great extent and it would have perhaps gone further. But in order that the process may be complete, it is necessary that a change in the Mahomedan mentality should come. The conflict is in the way of life and unless the Mahomedans learn tolerance I do not think the assimilation is possible. The Hindu is ready to tolerate. He is open to new ideas and his culture has got a wonderful capacity for assimilation, but always provided that India's central truth is recognized.

—Aurobindo Ghosh

~***~

Astrology: I know nothing of the science of astrology and I consider it to be a science, if it is a science, of doubtful value, to be severely left alone by those who have any faith in providence.

—Mahatma Gandhi

~***~

At peace: That one is blessed and at peace, who doesn't hope, to whom desire makes no more loans. Nothing coming, nothing owed.

—Lal Ded

~***~

Attachment: The less the thought of the body, the better it is. For, it is the body that drags us down. It is attachment and identifying, which makes us miserable.

—Swami Vivekananda

~***~

Attachment: But then, don't remain attached; learn to detach your mind from your work at a moment's notice. But this detachment is not indifference.

—Sri Sri Ravishankar

~***~

Attachment: He who is overly attached to his family members, experiences fear and sorrow, for the root of all grief is attachment. Thus, one should discard attachment to be happy.

—Chanakya

~***~

Attachment: Once one chooses the spiritual path, he must give up attachment to family and relatives; otherwise, he will not be able to progress. If a boat is anchored, one will not row in vain; the boat will not move forward. You have dedicated your lives to God; you must have strong faith that He will look after your family.

—Amritanandamayi

~***~

Attachment, non-attachment: When there is attachment to saints, there comes non-attachment. When there is non-attachment, there comes absence of delusion. When there is absence of delusion, there comes steadiness. When there is steadiness, there comes liberation in life.

—Adi Shankaracharya

~***~

Authors: It is the privilege of authors that they can help mankind endure adversities so they succeed in life.

—A.P.J. Abdul Kalam

~***~

Aversion: We should not dislike those who do immoral acts. Our aversion should be towards their deeds, not towards them.

—Mata Amritanandamayi

~***~

Avidyaa: *Avidyaa* (illusion and ignorance) is to be dispelled, and *Vidyaa* (realisation and acquisition of knowledge) should be promoted.

—Swami Dayanand Saraswati

~***~

Adversities: In all adversities, there is always in its depth, a treasure of spiritual blessings secretly hidden.

—Swami Chinmayananda

~***~

Awakening from sleep: The serpent, the king, the tiger, the stining wasp, the small child, the dog owned by other people, and the food: these seven ought not to be awakened from sleep.

—Chanakya

~***~

Awareness: Since it is awareness that makes consciousness possible, there is awareness in every state of consciousness. Therefore, the very consciousness of being conscious is already a movement in awareness. Interest in your stream of consciousness takes you to awareness. It is not a new state. It is at once recognized as the original, basic existence, which is life itself, and also love and joy.

—Nisargadatta Maharaj

~***~

Awareness of sleep: By eliminating the intervals of inadvertence during the waking hours, you will gradually eliminate the long interval of absent-mindedness, which you call sleep. You will be aware that you are asleep.

—*Nisargadatta Maharaj*

❑

B

Basic factors: The four basic factors that I am convinced are involved in successful missions: goal setting, positive thinking, visualising and believing.

—A.P.J. Abdul Kalam

~***~

Beast: Every species, human and sub-human, has some distinguishing mark, so that you can tell a man from a beast, or a dog from a cow.

—Mahatma Gandhi

~***~

Beautiful minds: Beautiful minds are the source of creativity.

—A.P.J. Abdul Kalam

~***~

Being: Love is not just an emotion. It is the very state of your being.

—Sri Sri Ravishankar

~***~

Beauty: Beauty doesn't need ornaments. Softness can't bear the weight of ornaments.

—Munshi Premchand

~***~

Beauty: Beauty is truth's smile when she beholds her

own face in a perfect mirror.

—Rabindranath Tagore

~***~

Bed of nails: You don't have to lie on a bed of nails in order to meditate; you may sit on a cushioned chair, if you wish. Externals are not important. The Lord looks into your mind and heart. If you are sincere in your desire for him, he will reveal himself to you.

—Swami Prabhavananda

~***~

Bee: The bee gathers honey without injuring the scent or the colour of the flower. So should a silent one (Muni) live his life.

—Dhammapada

~***~

Beginning of awakening: What obstruct one on the spiritual path bears within itself seeds of future suffering. Yet the heartache, the anguish over the effect of these obstructions, are the beginning of an awakening to consciousness.

—Amritanandamayi Mata

~***~

Before more powerful: Before advancing against men weaker than yourself, ponder when you stood before those more powerful.

—Thirukkı.ral

~***~

Behaviour: Do to others what you would have them do to you. The source of the famous Golden Rule.

—Matthew 7:12

~***~

Being fascinated: Why do I find pleasure in the fleeting things of this world?" If you crave for some outer thing or feel very attracted to a person, you should pause and say to yourself: Look out, you are being fascinated by the glamour of this!" Is there a place where God is not?

—Sri Anandamayi Ma

~***~

Belief: Man is made by his belief. As he believes, so he is.

—Bhagavad Gita

~***~

Belief: Whatever you believe to be, that you will be. If you believe yourselves to be sages, sages you will be tomorrow. There is nothing to obstruct you.

—Swami Vivekananda

~***~

Believe in ourselves: If we do not believe in ourselves and do not develop our technologies and work with them, the same thing will come to us from other countries with an alienated majesty. If we trust ourselves and rely on our own wisdom, technological dependence would be a thing of the past.

—A.P.J. Abdul Kalam

~***~

Best of men: Do not be friends of evil doers or of mean men. Do be friends with the good; keep company with the best of men.

—Dhammapada

~***~

Best: Do the best and leave the rest.

—Swami Chinmayananda

~***~

Beyond: That which is beyond speech, cannot be spoken of, nor written down on paper.

—Sant Namdev

~***~

Bhagavad Gita: From a clear knowledge of the Bhagavad Gita, all the goals of human existence become fulfilled. Bhagavad Gita is the manifest quintessence of all the teachings of the Vedic scriptures.

—Adi Shankaracharya

~***~

Bhagavad Gita: The Bhagavad Gita was spoken by Lord Krishna to reveal the science of devotion to God, which is the essence of all spiritual knowledge.

—Ramanuja

~***~

Bhakti: It does not matter if your *bhakti* is imperfect. Perform *bhakti*! Radhasoami [the Lord of the Soul] graciously declares that you should perform *bhakti* in whichever way you can. Fear not. He will grant you the Treasure of Love. You will be a recipient of the Gift of Love.

—Swami Ji Maharaj, Sar Bachan

~***~

Biggest power: The world's biggest power is the youth and beauty of a woman.

—Chanakya

~***~

Bitter truth: There is some self-interest behind every friendship. There is no friendship without self-interest. This is a bitter truth.

—Chanakya

~***~

Blame: We have to go back to philosophy to treat things as they are. We are suffering from our own *karmas*. It is not the fault of God. What we do is our own fault, nothing else. Why should God be blamed?

—Swami Vivekananda

~***~

Blame: Why do those, whose life is devoid of renown, blame enemies who hate them, when they have themselves to blame?

—Thirukkural

~***~

Blessed, beautiful place: Wherever the Lord's Bhagat, a devotee goes, is a blessed, beautiful place.

—***Guru Granth Saheb***

~ * * * ~

Blessing: Don't think a Guru or a Master is always blessing. There are certain moments when that blessing flows with great force. Those are very precious moments to sit and receive that.

—***Sri Sri Ravishankar***

~ * * * ~

Bliss: Where there is FAITH, there is LOVE; Where there is LOVE, there is PEACE; Where there is PEACE, there is GOD; Where there is GOD, there is BLISS.

—***Sathya Sai Baba***

~ * * * ~

Blows: Blows are what awaken us and help to break the dream. They show us the insufficiency of this world and make us long to escape, to have freedom.

—***Swami Vivekananda***

~ * * * ~

Body and self: Does an ornament exist apart from the gold of which it is made? Where is the body apart from the Self? He who considers the body to be himself is an ignorant man. He who regards himself as the Self is the enlightened One who has realised the Self.

—***Ramana Maharshi***

~ * * * ~

Body and soul: As long as your body is healthy and under control and death is distant, try to save your soul; when death is imminent, what can you do?

—***Chanakya***

~ * * * ~

Body consciousness: To cease to be identified with the body, to separate oneself from the body-consciousness, is a recognized and necessary step whether towards spiritual liberation or toward spiritual perfection and mastery over Nature.

—Aurobindo Ghosh

~***~

Burden: Things in which we do not take joy are either a burden upon our minds to be got rid of at any cost.

—Rabindranath Tagore

~***~

Body: Tonight, when you go to sleep, feel your whole body. As you start feeling your body, you'll see you are not the body. You are a glow, you are consciousness. You are that scintillating energy, sparkling energy in the whole body.

—Sri Sri Ravishankar

~***~

Bondage: Desire, ignorance, and inequality—this is the trinity of bondage.

—Swami Vivekananda

~***~

Bondage: If you think that you are bound, you remain bound; you make your own bondage. If you know that you are free, you are free this moment. This is knowledge, knowledge of freedom. Freedom is the goal of all nature.

—Swami Vivekananda

~***~

Book: A good book is a source of great knowledge and wealth for many generations.

—A.P.J. Abdul Kalam

~***~

Book of nature: The book one must read to learn natural sciences is the book of nature. The book from which to learn religion is your own mind and heart.

—Swami Vivekananda

~***~

Books: Books are as useful to a stupid person as a mirror is useful to a blind person.

—***Chanakya***

~***~

Books: Four books in my life have been very close to my heart. I cherish reading them: They are—*Man, the Unknown, Thirukkural, Light from Many Lamps* and *The Holy Quran*.

—***A.P.J. Abdul Kalam***

~***~

Boots: Shri Paramhans (smiling): Bankim! Well, what has made you bent?" BANKIM (smiling): Why, sir, boots are responsible for it. The kicks of our white masters have bent my body.

—***Anonymous***

~***~

Boundaries: The current of the world has its boundaries, otherwise, it could have no existence, but its purpose is not shown in the boundaries which restrain it, but in its movement, which is towards perfection.

—***Rabindranath Tagore***

~***~

Brahman: All this is Brahman. Let a man meditate on that (visible world) as beginning, ending, and breathing in it (the Brahman).

—***Chandogya Upanishad***

~***~

Breath of life: Freedom is never dear at any price. It is the breath of life. What would a man not pay for living?

—***Mahatma Gandhi***

~***~

But truth: All the religions of the world, while they may differ in other respects, unitedly proclaim that nothing lives in this world but Truth.

—***Mahatma Gandhi***

~***~

Breathe success: Breathe success. I want the youngsters to dream and aim high and work for the country's transformation.

—A.P.J. Abdul Kalam

~***~

Breeze of grace: The breeze of grace is always blowing, but you have to set your sail to catch that breeze of grace.

—Swami Prabhavananda

~***~

Broad vision: Soft-brained, weak-minded, chicken-hearted people cannot find the truth. One has to be free, and as broad as the sky.

—Swami Vivekananda

~***~

Butterfly: The butterfly counts not months but moments, and has time enough.

—Rabindranath Tagore

~***~

Brotherhood: Brotherhood is an ideal better understood by example than precept!

—Paramahansa Yogananda

❑

C

Calmness: Let the mind be cheerful and calm. Never let it run into excesses, because every excess will be followed by a reaction.

—Swami Vivekananda

~***~

Candle: A candle loses nothing by lighting another candle.

— A.P.J. Abdul Kalam

~***~

Candle: If you can't become a star in the sky, at least, become a candle in the darkness.

—Rabindranath Tagore

~***~

Candle: It is better to light one candle than to curse the darkness.

—Emerson

~***~

Capacity: Everything comes to us that belongs to us if we create the capacity to receive it.

—Rabindranath Tagore

~***~

Central core: Whatever action you do, whatever events

happen around you, it does not touch a central point of your life. That central core of your life remains a virgin.

—Sri Sri Ravishankar

~***~

Cessation of awareness: It is the cessation of the awareness of action and of experience, the giving up of conditioning and, thus, the attainment of peace and the state of equilibrium, that is known by the expression 'abandonment of action'.

—Yoga Vashishta

~***~

Calamity, discrimination: When calamity approaches, discrimination departs.

—Sathya Sai Baba

~***~

Change: All things in creation are subject to the law of change, and man, too, is subject to this law.

—Sathya Sai Baba

~***~

Change: If you want your life to change, your choices and actions must change. Everyday brings a chance to start over.

—Anonymous

~***~

Change: "Whatever's happened is for the good. Whatever's yet to happen is for the good. Whatever's not happened, that too is for the good. To grieve, what have you brought with you. Whatever you have gained, you have taken from here. Yesterday, it was somebody else's. Now it is yours. And tomorrow, it will be somebody else's. Change is the Nature of the world.

—Osho

~***~

Chaos and sorrow: The entire purpose of a clean and well-ordered life is to liberate man from the thraldom of chaos and the burden of sorrow.

—Nisaragadatta Maharaj

~***~

Character: Character is formed from the repeated choice of thoughts and action. Make the right choice—You shall have a firm and noble character.

—***Swami Chinmayananda***

~***~

Character: It is easy to do great deeds, the deeds that bring name and fame. But it is by his small everyday actions, that a person's character is known.

—***Swami Prabhavananda***

~***~

Character: When we can attach the mind to, or detach it from, the sense at our will, we shall really possess character. Then alone we shall have taken a long step towards freedom; before that, we are mere machines.

—***Swami Vivekananda***

~***~

Charnel pit: Kites and vultures soar very high indeed, but their gaze is fixed only on the charnel pit. The pundit has no doubt studied many books and scriptures;. but if he is attached to women, if he thinks of money and honour as the essential things, will you call him a pundit?

—***Ramkrishna Paramhansa***

~***~

Cheapest commodity: God is the cheapest commodity available, because outside of God, there can be nothing. There is no 'outside' at all.

—***Sri Sri Ravishankar***

~***~

Child of God: I am child of God. I am greater than anything that can happen to me.

—***A.P.J. Abdul Kalam***

~***~

Children: Children are living beings—more living than grown-up people, who have built shells of habit around themselves. Therefore, it is absolutely necessary for their mental health and development that they should not have mere schools for their lessons, but a world, whose guiding spirit is personal love.

—Rabindranath Tagore

~***~

Children: How can the devotees really have any caste? Children are all equal.

—Sharda Devi

~***~

Children: The child learns so easily because he has a natural gift, but adults, because they are tyrants, ignore natural gifts and say that children must learn through the same process that they learned by.

—Rabindranath Tagore

~***~

Christ: Christ has been much misinterpreted by the world. Even the most elementary principles of his teachings have been desecrated, and their esoteric depths have been forgotten. They have been crucified at the hands of dogma, prejudice and cramped understanding.

—Paramahansa Yogananda

~***~

Civilisation: Civilisation is intended to make us aware of the creativity in us.

—Dr. S. Radhakrishnan

~***~

Clamour of silence: Man goes into the noisy crowd to drown his own clamour of silence.

—Rabindranath Tagore

~***~

Comfort: Comfort – comes as guest, lingers to become host and stays to enslave us.

—Swami Chinmayananda

~***~

Company: Bad company is a company that disturbs the coolness, simplicity and innocence in you. Company that robs the joy from you is a bad company. Company that stimulates passion and ambition in you is a bad company.

—Sri Sri Ravishankar

~***~

Company: He who consorts with fools experiences great grief. The company of fools is like company of enemies—productive of pain. Company of the wise is like meeting of real kinsfolk—it brings happiness.

—Dhammapada

~***~

Compassion: How can one, who eats the flesh of others to swell his flesh, show compassion?

—Thirukkural

~***~

Compassion: If you want others to be happy, practise compassion. If you want to be happy, practise compassion.

—Dalai Lama

~***~

Compassion: Compassion is not religious business, it is human business, it is not luxury, it is essential for our own peace and mental stability, it is essential for human survival.

—Dalai Lama

~***~

Competitiveness: Competitiveness has three dimensions—quality, cost and just-in-time in market. Competitiveness is the common factor between the developed and developing countries. Competitiveness is the crown in the kingdom of sweat.

—A.P.J. Abdul Kalam

~***~

Competitiveness: The competitiveness is powered by knowledge power. The knowledge power is powered by technology and innovation.

—A.P.J. Abdul Kalam

~***~

Concentration: One who has not desisted from bad conduct, whose senses are not under control, whose mind is not concentrated, whose mind is not free from anxiety (about the result of concentration), cannot attain this self through knowledge.

—Katha Upanishad

~***~

Concubinage and polygamy: No words can adequately express the great and many evils of polygamy and concubinage, and especially as a source of misery to a Muslim woman. Take the caste system. Everybody infers that Islam must be free from slavery and caste. [While slavery existed], much of its support was derived from Islam and Islamic countries. While the prescriptions by the Prophet regarding the just and humane treatment of slaves contained in the Koran are praiseworthy, there is nothing whatever in Islam that lends support to the abolition of this curse. But if slavery has gone, caste among *Musalmans* [Muslims] has remained.

—B.R. Ambedkar

~***~

Confession of errors: Confession of errors is like a broom, which sweeps away the dirt and leaves the surface brighter and clearer. I feel stronger for confession.

—Mahatma Gandhi

~***~

Creeds: Are creeds such simple things like the clothes, which a man can change at will and put on at will? Creeds are such for which people live for ages and ages.

—Mahatma Gandhi

~***~

Course of history: A small body of determined spirits fired by an unquenchable faith in their mission can alter the course of history.

~***~

—Mahatma Gandhi

Compromise: A principle is the expression of perfection, and as imperfect beings like us cannot practise perfection, we devise every moment limits of its compromise in practice.

—*Mahatma Gandhi*

~***~

Confusion: Be alert. Question, observe, investigate, learn all you can about confusion, how it operates, what it does to you and others. By being clear about confusion, you become clear of confusion.

—*Nisargadatta Maharaj*

~***~

Conquest: A conquest, without facing dangers is, as dull as victory without a shining glory. A game without a prize!

—*Swami Chinmayananda*

~***~

Consciousness: Consciousness is eternal; it is not vanquished with the destruction of the temporary body.

—*Bhagvad Gita*

~***~

Consciousness: Krishna Consciousness is so nice that if one takes part in it in either ways, like hearing, chanting, remembering, worshipping, praying, or even simply by eating prasadam, the transcendental effect will be visible.

—*Srila Prabhupada*

~***~

Consciousness of immortality: Know that this universe is nothing but a dream bluff of nature to test your consciousness of immortality.

—*Paramahansa Yogananda*

~***~

Counsel: Where no counsel is, the people fall: but in the multitude of counsellers, there is safety.

—*Advice. Proverbs (ch. XI, v. 14)*

~***~

Consideration: Whatever creature comes to you, human or otherwise, treat it with consideration.

—*Shirdi Sai Baba*

~***~

Contagion: Like timidity, bravery is also contagious.

—Munshi Premchand

~***~

Contradictions: What is supremely important is to be free from contradictions; the goal and the way must not be on different levels; life and light must not quarrel; behaviour must not betray belief.

—Nisargadatta Maharaj

~***~

Cords of death: He is indeed the guardian of this world in time, the Lord of all, hidden in all things. In Him are united the seers of Brahman as well as the gods. By knowing Him, one cuts the cords of death.

—Svetasvatara Upanishad

~***~

Coward: A coward is incapable of exhibiting love; it is the prerogative of the brave.

—Mahatma Gandhi

~***~

Craving: Every experience, when it is overdone, every sense, brings nausea. Craving turns into aversion. And aversion continues, then it turns into craving. With this feverishness of aversion and craving, the mind gets clogged, closed—it's unable to see the light deep within.

—Sri Sri Ravishankar

~***~

Create a purpose: Stop looking for a purpose as to why you are here. Create it.

—Osho

~***~

Creation: Our creation is the modification of relationship.

—Rabindranath Tagore

~***~

Creation and destruction: Creation and destruction are two sides of the same coin. They almost happen simultaneously—the moment you are born, you are also dying.

—Sri Sri Ravishankar

~***~

Creation's waves: I, the ocean of mind, drink all creation's waves. Eternity and I, one united ray. I, a tiny bubble of laughter, Have become the Sea of Mirth Itself.

—Paramahansa Yogananda

~***~

Creative: Competition destroys creativity; but you have been told the other way round. People have always told you that you have to be competitive, that you should win over the competition, otherwise you can't survive. No — if you want to be creative, you shouldn't be competitive.

—Sri Sri Ravishankar

~***~

Creative urge: Whenever our life is stirred by truth, it expresses energy and comes to be filled, as it were, with a creative ardour. This consciousness of the creative urge is evidence of the force of truth on our mind.

—Rabindranath Tagore

~***~

Creativity: Creativity is seeing the same thing as everybody else, but thinking of out-of-the-box solutions.

—A.P.J. Abdul Kalam

~***~

Crossing the sea: You can't cross the sea merely by standing and staring at the water. Don't let yourself indulge in vain wishes.

—Rabindranath Tagore

~***~

Cultivation of mind: Cultivation of mind should be the ultimate aim of human existence.

—B.R. Ambedkar

~***~

Cultured, uncultured: The cultured give happiness

wherever they go. The uncultured, whenever they go!

—Swami Chinmayananda

~***~

Cultures: Cultures are like many-hued glasses. Just as these glasses make colourless light to assume colour for them, cultures colour human essence.

—A.P.J. Abdul Kalam

~***~

Cunning: Everyone is busy using his cunning. None plays the game with the detachment that can cure the fever within.

—Sant Namdev

~***~

Creator: You are the Creator, you alone are my friend, You, O Lord, are all-pervading. True meditation reveals You in all Your perfection; And the snares of illusion are rendered ineffective.

—Sant Namdev

~***~

Current: The same current activates all.

—Sathya Sai Baba

~***~

Curse: Her (India's) great curse is caste; but English education has already proved a tremendous power in levelling the injurious distinctions of caste.

—Keshub Chander Sen

~***~

Curses: Let them through their curses. If inside I am connected to what's true, my soul stays quiet and clear. Do you think Shiva worries what people say! If a few ashes fall on a mirror, use them to polish it.

—Lal Ded

❑

D

Death: Death is as sure for that which is born, as birth is for that which is dead. Therefore, grieve not for what is inevitable.

—Bhagavad Gita

~***~

Deed: For I verily, absent in body, but present in spirit, have judged already, as though I were present, concerning him that hath so done this deed.

—Corinthians (ch. V, v. 3)

~***~

Delusion: Delusion arises from anger. The mind is bewildered by delusion. Reasoning is destroyed when the mind is bewildered. One falls down when reasoning is destroyed.

—Bhagavad Gita

~***~

Delusions: From the viewpoint of absolute truth, what we feel and experience in our ordinary daily life is all delusion. Of all the various delusions, the sense of discrimination between oneself and others is the worst form, as it creates nothing but unpleasantness for both sides.

—Dalai Lama

~***~

Demonic qualities: Hypocrisy, arrogance, pride, anger, harshness, and ignorance; these are the marks of those who are born with demonic qualities.

—Bhagavad Gita

~***~

Desire: The desire has driven you crazy. Stop for a while and look at it: 'What is it?'—that feverishness dissolves and disappears, vanishes.

—Sri Sri Ravishankar

~***~

Desire: The fundamental desire of life is the desire to exist.

—Rabindranath Tagore

~***~

Desire for God: The main thing is to create the desire for God by reading scriptures, praying to God, chanting his praises. Eventually, there will come a time in your life when you feel that God alone is real, and you seek Him and Him only. Then you will find illumination.

—Swami Prabhavananda

~***~

Desires: Offer the desires that have already arisen in you, then also you'll become peaceful and happy—instantaneously.

—Sri Sri Ravishankar

~***~

Despondency: Despondency is not religion, whatever else it may be.

—Swami Vivekananda

~***~

Destiny: Each man carries his destiny in his own hands.

—Sathya Sai Baba

~***~

Destruction destroyed: Now you should understand that one who loves God is but out to destroy identification with the body. When this has come about, there is destruction of delusion, of bondage in other words, of desire, of not-self.

—Sri Anandmayi Ma

~***~

Development: Constant development is the law of life, and a man, who always tries to maintain his dogmas in order to appear consistent, drives himself into a false position.

—Mahatma Gandhi

~***~

Devoted circle...wealth: As long as one is fond of acquiring wealth, so long one's circle is devoted. Later, one lives in a decrepit body, and none in the house inquires about one's well-being.

—Adi Shankaracharya

~***~

Devotee: Repeat constantly the Name of the Lord, and know that devotion indispensable for deliverance. Thus, the devotee becomes the Lord Himself, and, thus, has the Lord become Tuka.

—Sant Tukaram

~***~

Devotees: The wind of *Maya* blows and shakes us, but the Lord's devotees remain ever-stable. They remain unaffected by pleasure and pain.

—Guru Granth Saheb

~***~

Devotion: Devotion is not a uniform to be worn on certain days and then to be put aside.

—Sathya Sai Baba

~***~

Devotion: Life is given. Nothing is earned. So learn to serve others, not your own desire greed and ego. They steal your energies. Whereas devotion builds your strength and protects the intelligent flame that leads to the truth within.

—Lal Ded

~***~

Dewdrop: A dewdrop is a perfect integrity that has no filial memory of its parentage.

—Rabindranath Tagore

~***~

Dharma: All acts ought to be performed in conformity with *dharma* (Righteousness and Duty), i.e. after due consideration of the truth and the untruth.

—Swami Dayanand Saraswati

~***~

Demons: Men draw out their days polishing their exteriors. But crooked within their hearts are like demons.

—Sant Namdev

~***~

Dharma: It is *Dharma* which upholds, sustains, supports, and guides mankind to live a higher life irrespective of race, caste, class or faith.

—B.K.S. Iyengar

~***~

Difference: You are me, and I am You—what is the difference between us? We are like gold and the bracelet, or water and the waves.

—Sant Ravidas

~***~

Different dress: The same God which came as Sri Krishna, came again as Christ and as other divine incarnations. He only chose a different dress.

—Swami Prabhavananda

~***~

Difficult: Difficult it is to obtain birth as a human being. Difficult it is to live the life of a man. Difficult it is to get to hear the True Law. Difficult it is to attain to Enlightenment.

—Dhammapada

~***~

Difficulties: Man needs his difficulties because they are necessary to enjoy success.

—A.P.J. Abdul Kalam

~***~

Difficulties of life: Difficulties of life may come as seasonal changes but we should not be disturbed by all those difficulties. Our process is to chant and that process will gradually clear everything in due course.

—Srila Prabuapada

~***~

Dignity: Courage of conviction gives us strength and dignity.

—A.P.J. Abdul Kalam

~***~

Disability: Perception of disability lies in the mind.

—A.P.J. Abdul Kalam

~***~

Discipline: Discipline is the mark of intelligent living.

—Sathya Sai Baba

~***~

Disease and cure: The world is my disease, and You are the cure. You. You.

—Lal Ded

~***~

Disgrace: To the honoured, dishonour is worse than death.

—Bhagavad Gita

~***~

Dislike or distrust: There should not be any trace of dislike or distrust on the score of nationality, language, caste, economic status, scholarship, age or sex.

—Sathya Sai Baba

~***~

Dispassion: Dispassion is not apathy. Often we think dispassion means being totally unenthusiastic, depressed, not interested in anything—this is not dispassion.

Dispassion is lack of feverishness.

—Sri Sri Ravishankar

~***~

Dispassion: You think dispassion means lack of joy. This is not so; dispassion is joy. Dispassion means 'full of joy.' When you say, 'I don't want anything,' that means you have everything.

—Sri Sri Ravishankar

~***~

Distinguish: Distinguish right from wrong and be honest, upright and virtuous.

—Shirdi Sai Baba

~***~

Disrespect: You should not stay for even one second at a place where people are speaking disrespectfully of a saint.

—Shirdi Sai Baba

~***~

Disunited mind: The disunited mind is far from wise; how can it meditate? How be at peace? When you know no peace, how can you know joy?

—Bhagavad Gita

~***~

Divine: If someone is beautiful, that beauty is bestowed by the Divine, it belongs to the Divine. If someone is educated, that knowledge is bestowed by the Divine. Someone is doing some good or bad actions, those actions are from the Divine.

—Sri Sri Ravishankar

~***~

Divine: See the divine in the human being.

—Shirdi Sai Baba

~***~

Divinity: Manifest the divinity within you. Everything will be harmoniously arranged around it.

—Swami Vivekananda

~***~

Doctrines, false: They who fear when there is no cause for fear [as well as] they who do not fear when they ought to fear—both enter the downward path, following false doctrines.

—Dhammapada

~***~

Doubt: I have tried many methods, but by turning it away, the noose of doubt is not turned away.

—Sant Ravidas

~***~

Doubter: There is neither this world nor the world beyond nor happiness for the one who doubts.

—Bhagavad Gita

~***~

Dream: Dream leads to the development of a nation. Dreams transform into thoughts; thoughts result into actions. Great dreams of great dreamers are always fascinating. We must think and act like a nation of a billion people and not like that of a million people. Dream, dream, dream!

—A.P.J. Abdul Kalam

~***~

Dream: You have to dream before your dreams can come true.

—A.P.J. Abdul Kalam

~***~

Duality: Duality—a divided mind—is the cause of fear and misery.

—Sri Sri Ravishankar

~***~

Due: We should give everyone his due. What is not edible for a man, give to a cow; what is not edible for a cow, give to a dog; what is not edible for a dog, throw into a lake for fishes to eat. But never waste.

—Sarada Devi

~***~

Duty: Perform your obligatory duty, because action is indeed better than inaction.

—Bhagavad Gia

~***~

Duty: What is our duty? To behave properly. That is enough.

—Shirdi Sai Baba

❑

E

Eating: One person can eat meat and become absorbed in God, and another can eat vegetables and be a rogue. If you consider vegetarianism from the standpoint of non-killing, remember that even potatoes have life. So, I would say, eat what agrees with you and what you can digest.

—*Swami Prabhavananda*

~***~

Eating wih a ruler: When thou sittest to eat with a ruler, consider diligently what is before thee: And put a knife to thy throat, if thou be a man given to appetite.

—*Proverbs (ch. 23, v. 1-2)*

~***~

Education, character: Education is the chief remedy for all those great evils which afflict the country. Education will not only cultivate and improve the intellect of the nation, but will also purify its character.

—*Keshub Chander Sen*

~***~

Education, conventional: Conventional education makes independent thinking extremely difficult. Conformity leads to mediocrity. To be different from the group or to resist environment is not easy and is often risky. The urge to be successful, which is the pursuit of reward whether in the material or in the so-called spiritual sphere, the search for inward or outward security, the desire for comfort this whole process smothers discontent, puts an end to spontaneity and breeds fear; and fear blocks the intelligent understanding of life.

—J. Krishnamurthy

~***~

Education: Education is the best friend. An educated person is respected everywhere. Education beats the beauty and the youth.

—Chanakya

~***~

Education: Education should be imparted with a view to the type of society that we wish to build.

— A.P.J. Abdul Kalam

~***~

Education: The highest education is that which does not merely give us information but makes our life in harmony with all existence.

—Rabindranath Tagore

~***~

Education: When the nation is progressing towards economic development, it is also essential to build education with value system drawn from our civilisational heritage.

—A.P.J. Abdul Kalam

~***~

Education: The object of education is to give man the unity of truth.

—Rabindranath Tagore

~***~

Education, literacy: To be successful in life what you need is education, not literacy and degrees.

—Munshi Premchand

~***~

Effectiveness: Become quietly effective.

—Swami Chinmayananda

~***~

Ego: It is more than ever necessary to keep yourself free from all taint of the perversions of the ego.

—Aurobindo Ghosh

~***~

Ego: Take out the thorn of the ego. Take out the name and the shape and there is nothing. You see by your own understanding that everything is illusion. Experience it! You don't want to see because the mind doesn't allow you to see.

—Ranjit Maharaj

~***~

Ego: When there is Love, there is no ego; ego dissolves like the dewdrops with the sun.

—Sri Sri Ravishankar

~***~

Egotism: Do not be obsessed by egotism, imagining that you are the cause of action: everything is due to God.

—Shirdi Sai Baba

~***~

Elation: Good people move onwards whatever befall. They do not prattle, nor yearn for pleasures. The wise are not elated in their happiness, nor are they depressed when touched by sorrow.

—Dhammapada

~***~

Emancipation: The emancipation of our physical nature is in attaining health, of our social being in attaining goodness, and of our self in attaining love.

—Rabindranath Tagore

~***~

Emotional energy: Man has a fund of emotional energy, which is not all occupied with his self-preservation. This surplus seeks its outlet in the creation of art, for man's civilization is built upon his surplus.

—Rabindranath Tagore

~***~

End and means: What is material and what is not material? When the world is the end and God the means to attain that end, then that is material. When God is the end and the world is only the means to attain that end, spirituality has begun.

—Swami Vivekananda

~***~

Enemy best teacher: In the practice of tolerance, one's enemy is the best teacher.

—Dalai Lama

~***~

Englishmen, caste affected: I was also pained to notice an institution which I certainly did not expect to find in this country—I mean *caste*. Your rich people are really Brahmins, and your poor people are Sudras.

—Keshub Chander Sen

~***~

Entrepreneur: Diversity of skills and perseverance in work makes an entrepreneur. The key characteristics required in an entrepreneur are desire, drive, discipline and determination.

—A.P.J. Abdul Kalam

~***~

Erring: To err is human; but how few know to lead an erring man?

—Sarada Devi

~***~

Erroneous assumption: It is an erroneous assumption of limited minds that great ones such as Jesus, Krishna, and other divine incarnations are gone from the earth when they are no longer visible to human sight. This is not so. They are very much alive and active today. In Spirit and occasionally taking on a flesh-and-blood form, they are working unseen by the masses for the regeneration of the world.

—Paramahansa Yogananda

~***~

Errors: If you shut your door to all errors, truth will be shut out.

—Rabindranath Tagore

~***~

Essence: Books are infinite in number and time is short. The secret of knowledge is to take that is essential. Take that and try to live up to it.

—Swami Vivekananda

~***~

Essenceless dream perception: Who are you? Who am I? Wherefrom have I come? Who is my mother? Who is my father? Reflect over this, having left aside all the universe which is an essenceless dream perception.

—Adi Shankaracharya

~***~

Essentials: Purity, patience and perseverance are the three essentials to success and, above all, there is love.

—Swami Vivekananda

~***~

Eternal: The Eternal which dwells in the soul has to be known. Beyond that there is nothing else to be known. By knowing the enjoyer, the object of enjoyment and the ruler, everything has been said. This is the three-fold Brahman.

—Svetasvatara Upanishad

~***~

Eternal life: In our desire for eternal life, we pray for an eternity of our habit and comfort, forgetting that immortality is in repeatedly transcending the definite forms of life in order to pursue the infinite truth of life.

—Rabindranath Tagore

~***~

Eternal now: Since past and future have never been without the present, to know the Eternal Now is to know the truth. The changeless, infinite Self transcends time and space, which are relative to the body and the mind.

—Ramana Rishi

~***~

Europe: Europe where men have constantly fought, killed, burned, tortured, imprisoned, persecuted in every way imaginable by human stupidity and cruelty for the sake of dogmas, words, rites and forms of church government, Europe where these things have done duty for spirituality and religion, has hardly a record, which would entitle it to cast this reproach in the face of the East....

—***Aurobindo Ghosh***

~***~

Evaluation: Don't evaluate yourself. When you stop evaluating yourself, that in itself is a sign of progress.

—***Sri Sri Ravishankar***

~***~

Everything well: Always aim at complete harmony of thought and word and deed. Always aim at purifying your thoughts and everything will be well.

—***Mahatma Gandhi***

~***~

Evil: They who discern evil where there is no evil [as well as] they who see nothing evil in what is evil—both enter the downward path, following false doctrines.

—***Dhammapada***

~***~

Evil: When you feel you cannot do good, at least, desist from doing evil.

—***Sathya Sai Baba***

~***~

Evil and imperfection: The question why there is evil in existence is the same as why there is imperfection.... But the real question is: Is this imperfection the final truth, is evil absolute and ultimate?

—***Rabindranath Tagore***

~***~

Evil and truth: Evil spreads with the wind; truth is capable of spreading even against it.

—***Paramahansa Yogananda***

~***~

Equanimity: Take failure and victory coolly.

—*Sathya Sai Baba*

~***~

Exercise in discrimination: Deliberate daily exercise in discrimination between the true and the false and renunciation of the false is meditation.

—*Nisargadatta Maharaj*

~***~

Existence: I exist without the cosmic shadow But it could not live bereft of me; As the sea exists without the waves, But they breathe not without the sea.

—*Paramahansa Yogananda*

~***~

Existence: That I exist is a perpetual surprise, which is life.

—*Rabindranath Tagore*

~***~

Existence: The potentiality of perfection outweighs actual contradictions.... Existence in itself is here to prove that it cannot be an evil.

—*Rabindranath Tagore*

~***~

Existence, mystery of: There is a point where in the mystery of existence contradictions meet; where movement is not all movement and stillness is not all stillness; yet not losing its infinity. If this meeting is dissolved, then things become unreal.

—*Rabindranath Tagore*

~***~

Existing: A man can close his eyes and realize that he exists, even though his body is invisible to his physical eyes and is present only as an idea.

—*Paramahansa Yogananda*

~***~

Experience: Experience stands between faith and falsehood.

—A.P.J. Abdul Kalam

~***~

Experience: Experience is the only teacher we have. We may talk and reason all our lives, but we shall not understand a word of truth until we experience it ourselves.

—Swami Vivekananda

~***~

Experience and health: Every experience that is drawn through any of the senses has an effect on one's health.

—Sathya Sai Baba

~***~

Extraordinary: Surely, life is not merely a job, an occupation; life is something extraordinarily wide and profound, it is a great mystery, a vast realm in which we function as human beings.

—J. Krishnamurthy

~***~

Eye for an eye: An eye for an eye only ends up making the whole world blind.

—Mahatma Gandhi

□

F

Facts and truth: Facts are many, but the truth is one.

—*Rabindranath Tagore*

~***~

Failure: Once you start working on something, don't be afraid of failure and don't abandon it. People who work sincerely are the happiest.

—*Chanakya*

~***~

Fair and guarded: Be fair in your judgement, and guarded in your speech.

—*Baha'u'llah*

~***~

Faith: Have faith in Guru, in his teachings, and in the surety that you can get free. Think day and night that this universe is zero, only God is there. Have intense desire to get free.

—*Swami Vivekananda*

~***~

Faith: So long as we believe in our heart of hearts that our capacity is limited and we grow anxious and unhappy, we are lacking in faith. One who truly trusts in God has no right to be anxious about anything.

—*Paramahansa Yogananda*

~***~

Faith, particular: If you have a particular faith or religion, that is good. If not, you can still live without it.

—Dalai Lama

~***~

Faith, steady: Steady faith is stronger than destiny. Destiny is the result of causes, mostly accidental, and is, therefore, loosely woven. Confidence and good hope will overcome it easily.

—Nisargadatta Maharaj

~***~

Faithful: The world cherishes faithful men who never forsake old friendships, worn by time but unbroken.

—Thirukkural

~***~

Familial connection: We are born and reborn countless number of times, and it is possible that each being has been our parent at one time or another. Therefore, it is likely that all beings in this universe have familial connections.

—Dalai Lama

~***~

Faults: Faults become thick when love is thin.

—Swami Chinmayananda

~***~

Faults: I look only to the good qualities of men. Not being faultless myself, I won't presume to probe into the faults of others.

—Mahatma Gandhi

~***~

Future: I do not want to foresee the future. I am concerned with taking care of the present. God has given me no control over the moment following.

—Mahatma Gandhi

~***~

Fear: Fear is fearful to approach Him.

—Swami Prabhavananda

~***~

Fear: As soon as the fear approaches near, attack and destroy it.

—Chanakya

~***~

Fear: Fear is death, fear is sin, fear is hell, fear is unrighteousness and fear is wrong life. All the negative thoughts and ideas that are in the world have proceeded from this evil spirit of fear.

—Swami Vivekananda

~***~

Fear: Fear there is not for him whose mind is not burning with desires, and which, having risen above likes and dislikes, is serene. He is awakened.

—Dhammapada

~***~

Fear: Those who own much have much to fear.

—Rabindranath Tagore

~***~

Fear and cowardice: Fear has its use but cowardice has none.

—Mahatma Gandhi

~***~

Fearless: Let us not pray to be sheltered from dangers but to be fearless when facing them.

—Rabindranath Tagore

~***~

Fearlessness: If there is one word that you find coming out like a bomb from the Upanishads, bursting like a bombshell upon masses of ignorance, it is the word 'fearlessness'.

—Swami Vivekananda

~***~

Feeling: Feel like Christ and you will be Christ, feel like the Buddha and you will be the Buddha. It is the feeling that is the life, the strength, the vitality, without which no amount of intellectual activity can reach God.

—*Swami Vivekananda*

~***~

Fetish: We cannot afford to raise any institution to the rank of a fetish. To do so would be simply to become the slaves of our own machinery.

—*Aurobindo Ghosh*

~***~

Final: Success or achievement is not the final goal. It is the 'spirit' in which you act that puts the seal of beauty upon your life.

—*Swami Chinmayananda*

~***~

Flaws: Do not judge. Just look at yourself—how many flaws you have. And Nature, the Divine, has accepted you with all your flaws.... It doesn't judge you at all.

—*Sri Sri Ravishankar*

~***~

Fleeing: Face the brutes. That is a lesson for all life. Face the terrible, face it boldly. Like the monkeys, the hardships of life fall back when we cease to flee before them.

—*Swami Vivekananda*

~***~

Flower: The picture of a flower in a botanical book is information; its mission ends with our knowledge. But in pure art, it is a personal communication.

—*Rabindranath Tagore*

~***~

Focus on spiritual development: By keeping our mind on God constantly, while engaged in any work, the benefit will reach all members of the family. The ultimate aim in life should not be to amass wealth for children and relatives; it should be to focus on our own spiritual development.

—*Amritanandamayi*

~***~

Foe: Call none a stranger, think none to be your foe.

—*Baha'u'llah*

~***~

Following God: There are so many religions and each one has its different ways of following God.

—*Mother Teresa*

~***~

Food: Food should not be too salty, too hot, too bitter, too sweet, too sour.

—*Sathya Sai Baba*

~***~

Food: Too much food results in dullness of mind.

—*Sathya Sai Baba*

~***~

Fool, folly: The fool aware of his folly is to that extent wise; but a fool who takes himself to be wise is a fool indeed.

—*Dhammapada*

~***~

Forbearing: Be not forbearing one with another, and set not your affections on things below. Pride not yourself in your glory, and be not ashamed of abasement. I have created all things from dust and to dust I will return them again.

—*Baha'u'llah*

~***~

Force of truth: Whenever our life is stirred by truth, it expresses energy and comes to be filled, as it were, with a creative ardour. This consciousness of the creative urge is evidence of the force of truth on our mind.

—*Rabindranath Tagore*

~***~

Forget: Prosperity is like wine, which goes to the head, and makes man forget his Creator.

—*Swami Chinmayananda*

~***~

Forget me not: Forget me not, O Mother, Should I fail to return To thy hallowed bossom. Make not the lotus of thy memory void of its nectar Madhu.

—Michael Madhusudan Dutt

~***~

Fragrance of virtuous: Faint is the scent of *tagara* or sandalwood. The fragrance of the virtuous ascends to the heights of the Gods.

—Dhammapada

~***~

Free of action: There are those sleeping who are awake, and others awake who are sound asleep. Some of those bathing in sacred pools will never get clear. And there are others doing household chores who are free of action.

—Lal Ded

~***~

Freedom: Not to do what you feel like doing is Freedom.

—Swami Chinmayananda

~***~

Freedom: To be capable of learning, the mind must put aside all that it has learnt, which is extraordinarily difficult.... When our mind is in a state of freedom, we want to find out, to understand or discover. That freedom is destroyed the moment we begin to interpret what we discover in terms of our conditioning, our established morality, environmental influences, and so on.

—J. Krishnamurthy

~***~

Freedom: Freedom, morality, and the human dignity of the individual consists precisely in this; that he does good not because he is forced to do so, but because he freely conceives it, wants it, and loves it.

—Mikhail Bakunin

~***~

Freedom, God's and your: The freedom that is yours in small things, God exercises in great ones. In both is He, in destruction and in construction. The history of nations, families and individuals is the great Lila (divine sport) that He stages with Himself.

—*Anandamayi Ma*

~***~

Friend and Foe: A man's ownself is his friend. A man's ownself is his foe.

—*Bhagavad Gita*

~***~

Friends: Choose friends who will stick to you till the end, through thick and thin.

—*Shirdi Sai Baba*

~***~

Friendship: An intimate of any strength will never listen to faults said of friends.

—*Anonymous*

~***~

Friendship: There cannot be friendship without equality. Exceptions are rare.

—*Swami Vivekananda*

~***~

Frog: The frog in the deep well knows nothing of its own country or other lands; just so, my mind, infatuated with corruption, understands nothing about this world or the next.

—*Sant Ravidas*

~***~

Fruits: When we rejoice in our fullness, then we can part with our fruits with joy.

—*Rabindranath Tagore*

~***~

Fundamentals: All compromise is based on give and take, but there can be no give and take on fundamentals. Any compromise on mere fundamentals is a surrender. For it is all give and no take.

—*Mahatma Gandhi*

~***~

Future: There is no destiny beyond and above ourselves; we are ourselves the architects of our future.

—Swami Chinmayananda

~***~

Future: To live only for some unknown future is superficial. Past meets the present and creates the future.

—A.P.J. Abdul Kalam

~***~

Future: They say that the bird and the *sannyasi* should not provide for the future. But the mother bird brings food in her mouth for her chicks; so she too provides. A householder needs money. He has to support his family.

—Ramakrishna Paramahansa

□

G

Gain: The greed of gain has no time or limit to its capaciousness. Its one object is to produce and consume.

—Rabindranath Tagore

~✻✻✻~

Gain: Before undertaking a project, ponder what will be gained, but the glory of the forbearing lasts until the end of time.

—Thirukkural

~✻✻✻~

Game: Make the whole life a game. There is no purpose, there is no aim, nothing. Just take it lightly, easily. Play the game. That is worship, that is celebration.

—Sri Sri Ravishankar

~✻✻✻~

Gandhi: Gandhi has sound economic and cultural reasons for encouraging the revival of cottage industries, but he does not counsel a fanatical repudiation of all modern progress. Machinery, trains, automobiles, the telegraph have played important parts in his own colossal life! Fifty years of public service, in prison and out, wrestling daily with practical details and harsh realities in the political world, have only increased his balance, open-mindedness, sanity, and humorous appreciation of the quaint human spectacle.

—Paramahansa Yogananda

~***~

Gandhi's experimentation with truth: Many ancient Indian masters have preached non-violence as a philosophy. Mahatma Gandhi, in this twentieth century, produced a very sophisticated approach because he implemented that very noble philosophy of non-violence in modern politics, and he succeeded. It has represented an evolutionary leap in political consciousness, his experimentation with truth.

—Dalai Lama

~***~

Gazing: What is happening in gazing? You are looking at somebody. For a few moments, you gaze with all your heart. Then, for a few moments, your mind is not running here and there. Then, you sit with eyes closed—the mind is completely settled.

—Sri Sri Ravishankar

~***~

Generosity: Gentleness, generosity and self-sacrifice are the exclusive possession of no one race or religion.

—Mahatma Gandhi

~***~

Generous and thankful: Be generous in prosperity and thankful in adversity.

—Baha'u'llah

~***~

Getting: What you sow, you reap. What you give, you get.

—Shirdi Sai Baba

~***~

Gift: A gift is pure when it is given from the heart to the right person at the right time and at the right place, and when we expect nothing in return.

—Bhagvad Gita

~***~

Gift: Accepting all conditions of life – whatever they may be—as His gift, abide in fortitude and do service.

—*Sri Anandamayi Ma*

~***~

Gita: A literal interpretation of the Gita lands one in a sea of contradictions.

—*Mahatma Gandhi*

~***~

Giving: We may often give without love, but we can never love without giving.

—*Swami Chinmayananda*

~***~

Glorious: The past was great no doubt, but I sincerely believe that the future will be more glorious still.

—*Swami Vivekananda*

~***~

Glory: Even flawlessly fruitful lands will lessen their yields when forced to support the body of one who lacks illustriousness.

—*Thirukkural*

~***~

Glory: Glory lies in the attempt to reach one's goal and not in reaching it.

—*Mahatma Gandhi*

~***~

Glory: In life, the glory lies not in the quarry, but in the chase.

—*Swami Chinmayananda*

~***~

Glory of life: The glory of life is not never falling. The true glory consists in rising each time we fall.

—*Swami Chinmayananda*

~***~

Glory of the forbearing: The gratification of the vengeful lasts only for a day.

—*Anonymous*

~***~

Grow into: Faith is not something to grasp, it is a state to grow into.

—Mahatma Gandhi

~***~

Goal of human life: One should identify one's *Atma*, beyond the three bodies (gross, subtle and causal), with Brahman (*Aksharbrahman*) and offer worship to *Parabrahman*. There is nothing greater than worshipping God.

—Swaminarayan

~***~

God: All roads lead to Rome if your destination is Rome. All roads and sects and denominations lead to God if your destination is God.

—Swami Prabhavananda

~***~

God: God is not so far away. He is not in the heavens above, nor in hell below. He is always near you.

—Shirdi Sai Baba

~***~

God: Every child comes with a message that God is not yet discouraged of man.

—Rabindranath Tagore

~***~

God: God finds himself by creating.

—Rabindranath Tagore

~***~

God: God is all Names and all forms.

—Sathya Sai Baba

~***~

God: God, Our Creator, has stored within our minds and personalities great potential, strength and ability. Prayer helps us tap and develop these powers.

—Anonymous

~***~

God: If God brings you to it, He will bring you through it. Happy moments, praise God; Difficult moments, seek

God; Quiet moments, worship God; Painful moments, trust God; Every moment, thank God.

—Sri Sri Ravishankar

~***~

God: To define God is to defile God.

—Swami Chinmayananda

~***~

God: God is not present in idols. Your feelings are your God. The soul is your temple.

—Chanakya

~***~

God: In waking, eating, working, dreaming, sleeping, serving, meditating, chanting, divinely loving, my soul constantly hums, unheard by any: God, God, God!

—Paramahansa Yogananda

~***~

God never laughs: To listen to some devout people, one would imagine that God never laughs.

—Aurobindo Ghosh

~***~

God's dwelling place: God's dwelling place is in the heart of man. The inner immortal soul and the great cosmic power are one and the same. Brahman is *Atman* and *Atman* is Brahman.

—Dr. S. Radhakrishnan

~***~

God's love: You know what the love of a father, or a mother, or a friend, or a sweetheart is. Any of these relationships may be established with God. On the human plane, these loves may fail you. But God is the one Person who will never fail you.

—Swami Prabhavananda

~***~

God's message: You, the human race, is the best of my creation.

—A.P.J. Abdul Kalam

~***~

God's promise: What has God promised? Strength for the day; rest for the labour done, light for the way.

—A.P.J. Abdul Kalam

~***~

Good company: Good company is important, it helps to cultivate good qualities.

—Sathya Sai Baba

~***~

Good: Do your little bit of good where you are; it's those little bits of good put together that overwhelm the world.

—Desmond Tutu

~***~

Good deeds: In battle, in the forest, at the precipice in the mountains, on the dark great sea, in the midst of javelins and arrows, in sleep, in confusion, in the depths of shame, the good deeds a man has done before defend him.

—Bhagvad Gita

~***~

Goodness: Goodness is a fundamental characteristic of essence. It is a timeless potential that might reveal itself at any point or any place. It is unblemished goodness, incorruptible goodness, indestructible goodness. It is not parcelled out to individuals. It is totally boundless, unlimited and endless.

—A.P.J. Abdul Kalam

~***~

Goodness: The fragrance of flowers spreads only in the direction of the wind. But the goodness of a person spreads in all directions.

—Chanakya

~***~

Goodness: No one can be good for long if goodness is not in demand.

—Brecht, Bertolt

~***~

Grace: Grace is only to be found by effort, although it is here and now.

—Swami Chinmayananda

~***~

Gratefulness: Gratefulness purifies your system.

—Sri Sri Ravishankar

~***~

Gratitude: Having slain every kind of goodness, one may yet escape, but there is no escape for those who let gratitude die.

—Thirukkural

~***~

Great: When it is said that India shall be great, it is the *Sanatan Dharma* that shall be great.

—Aurobindo Ghosh

~***~

Great deeds: It is easy to do great deeds, the deeds that bring name and fame. But it is by his small, everyday actions that a person's character is known.

—Swami Prabhavananda

~***~

Great events in history: There are four great events in history, the siege of Troy, the life and crucifixion of Christ, the exile of Krishna in Brindaban and the colloquy on the field of Kurukshetra. The siege of Troy created Hellas, the exile in Brindaban created devotional religion (for before there was only meditation and worship), Christ from his cross humanized Europe, the colloquy at Kurukshetra will yet liberate humanity.

—Aurobindo Ghosh

~***~

Great in humility: We come nearest to the great when we are great in humility.

—Rabindranath Tagore

~***~

Great minds: The great minds radiate knowledge, which attract young students to take difficult subjects and specialise with ease. The great minds of the country had the ability to make others join their endeavour to convert dreams into reality for them; the nation was bigger than them and they could draw thousands to act upon their dreams.

—A.P.J. Abdul Kalam

~***~

Great silence: The water in a vessel is sparkling; the water in the sea is dark. The small truth has words which are clear; the great truth has great silence.

—Rabindranath Tagore

~***~

Great, eminent: A great man is different from an eminent one in that he is ready to be the servant of the society.

—B.R. Ambedkar

~***~

Greatest happiness: To love and to be loved is the greatest happiness.

—Swami Chinmayananda

~***~

Greatest school: This earth is higher than all the heavens; this is the greatest school in the universe.

—Swami Vivekananda

~***~

Greatness: The greatness is not what we do, but, unavoidably, it is always in how we do what we do. Our present work may be great or small, yet, the important is to do it well.

—Swami Chinmayananda

~***~

Guardian: He is wise and righteous who guides others not by force and violence but equitably. He is the guardian of the Law.

—Dhammapada

~***~

Guides: You seek guides, masters, systems, because you hope that by following them, obeying them, imitating them you will have peace [and] comfort. They are the tricksters who become priests, exploiters, preachers, mediators, *swamis* and *yogis*.

—J. Krishnamurthy

~***~

Guiding light: Be eyes to the blind and a guiding light unto to the feet of the erring.

—Baha'u'llah

~***~

Guilty: When we think we know, we cease to learn. All of us are guilty of this sometimes, some of us are guilty of it all the time.

—Dr. S. Radhakrishnan

~***~

Gunatit Sadhu: The scriptures say that *nishkam, nirlobh, nirman, niswad* and *nissneh* are the attributes of a *Sadhu*. The *Sadhu,* in whom one observes such attributes has a constant rapport with God.

—Swaminarayan

~***~

Guru: The Guru is not a physical form. The Guru is not an impressive figure peering at you from a picture. The Guru is not a person with long hair or a beard. The Guru is the divine power of Grace. The Guru is *Shakti*.

—Swami Muktananda

❑

H

Hand: Whatsoever thy hand findeth to do, do it with thy might.

—*Ecclesiastes*

~***~

Handling: A blade of *kusa* grass wrongly handled cuts the hand; asceticism wrongly practised leads downward to hell.

—*Dhammapada*

~***~

Happy: There are two ways of being happy: We must either diminish our wants or augment our means—either may do—the result is the same and it is for each man to decide for himself and to do that which happens to be easier.

—*Franklin, Benjamin*

~***~

Happiness: Happiness is not something readymade. It comes from your own actions.

—*Dalai Lama*

~***~

Happiness: Do you want my one-word secret of happiness? It's growth—mental, financial, you name it.

—*Harold S. Geneen*

~***~

Happiness: Happiness is when what you think, what you say, and what you do are in harmony.

—*Mahatma Gandhi*

~***~

Happiness: If you want happiness for an hour—take a nap. If you want happiness for a day—go fishing. If you want happiness for a month—get married. If you want happiness for a year—inherit a fortune. If you want happiness for a lifetime—help someone else.

—*Chinese Proverb*

~***~

Happiness: Real happiness lies within you.

—*Sathya Sai Baba*

~***~

Happiness and peace: The happiness and peace attained by those satisfied by the nectar of spiritual tranquility is not attained by greedy persons restlessly moving here and there.

—*Chanakya*

~***~

Hard fact: This life is a hard fact. Work your way through it boldly, though it may be adamantine. No matter, the soul is stronger.

—*Swami Vivekananda*

~***~

Harmonious: The highest education is that which does not merely give us information but makes our life in harmony with all existence.

—*Rabindranath Tagore*

~***~

Harmony: Harmony knows only delight of creator.

—*A.P.J. Abdul Kalam*

~***~

Harmony: When there is harmony in the home, there will be order in the nation. When there is order in the nation, there will be PEACE in the world..

—Sathya Sai Baba

~***~

Hateful: If somebody is hateful, we can only have compassion for them, because they are not aware of the center; they have moved from their love.

—Sri Sri Ravishankar

~***~

Hatred: Be ashamed of your hatred. Give up hatred and be quiet.

—Shirdi Sai Baba

~***~

Hatred: He reviled me, he beat me and conquered and then plundered me, who do not express such thoughts, in them hatred will cease.

—Dhammapada

~***~

HE: If I say that He is within me, the universe is ashamed; if I say that He is without me, it is falsehood."

—Rabindranath Tagore

~***~

Head and heart: In life to handle yourself, use your head, but to handle others, use your heart.

—Swami Chinmayananda

~***~

Heal emotional: Take all the time you need to heal emotionally. Moving on doesn't take a day; it takes lots of little steps to be able to break free of your broken self.

—Anonymous

~***~

Health: To enjoy good health, to bring true happiness to one's family, to bring peace to all, one must first discipline and control one's own mind. If a man can control his mind, he can find the way to Enlightenment, and all wisdom and virtue will naturally come to him.

—Buddha

~***~

Heap of rubbish: From a heap of rubbish on the roadside, a lily blooms, fragrant and pleasing.

—Dhammapada

~***~

Hear and listen: To listen is not merely to hear. We in life hear but very rarely do we know how to listen. To listen is to hear, with an intellectual alertness and attention of awareness.

—Swami Chinmayananda

~***~

Heart: In the garden of thy heart plant naught but the rose of love, and from the nightingale of affection and desire loosen not thy hold.

—Baha'u'llah

~***~

Heart: Culture of the mind must be subservient to the heart.

—Mahatma Gandhi

~***~

Hearts: It's not worth living in this planet—walking, talking, eating, drinking, doing anything—if the heart is not opened. And 95% of the population, I could even say 99% of the population, dies without the heart being opened.

—Sri Sri Ravishankar

~***~

Heaven: Trees are Earth's endless effort to speak to the listening heaven.

—Rabindranath Tagore

~***~

Heaven: Heaven is within you, seek happiness not in the objects of sense; realize that happiness is within yourself.

—Swami Ram Tirath

~***~

Hell: Hell has three gates: lust, anger and greed.

—Bhagavad Gita

~***~

Hell: If we all just sit and think, 'What about me, what about me,' then that is the hell.

—Sri Sri Ravishankar

~***~

Help to become better: Before you speak, it is necessary for you to listen, for God speaks in the silence of the heart.

—Mother Teresa

~***~

Here and now: Christ didn't say that you have to die a physical death in order to attain perfection. But your ego must die and you have to be reborn in Spirit in order to enter into the Kingdom of God. The goal, as both Hindus and Buddhists emphasize, is to be realized here and now, in this very life.

—Swami Prabhavananda

~***~

Him: Let them try to imprison Him in temple, mosque and church! The seeing eye finds the Beloved's signs in every mote.

—Sant Kabir

~***~

Himself to himself: When the road ends, and the goal is gained, the pilgrim finds that he has travelled only from himself to himself.

—Sathya Sai Baba

~***~

Hindu culture: More high-reaching, subtle, many-sided, curious and profound than the Greek, more noble and humane than the Roman, more large and spiritual than the old Egyptian, more vast and original than any other Asiatic civilization, more intellectual than the European prior to the 18th century, possessing all that these had and more, it was the most powerful, self-possessed, stimulating and wide in influence of all past human cultures.

—Satyavrata R. Patel

~***~

Hindu Dharam: It is the Hindu religion only because the Hindu nation has kept it, because in this Peninsula, it grew up in the seclusion of the sea and the Himalayas. But it does not belong peculiarly and forever to a bounded part of the world.

—*Aurobindo Ghosh*

~***~

Hindu, English educated: Look at that young, active, energetic Hindu, who has received education in some English school or college. Yesterday what was he? An ignorant Indian. Today what is he? An active, intelligent, fine-looking, educated man. Tomorrow what is he? He has English books on one side, he has the dangerous bottle of whisky on the other side. What is he the next day? Oh sad catastrophe! The whole house mourns the death of the promising young man.

—*Keshub Chander Sen*

~***~

Hinduism: Hinduism is not just a faith. It is the union of reason and intuition that cannot be defined but is only to be experienced. Evil and error are not ultimate. There is no Hell, for that means there is a place where God is not, and there are sins which exceed his love.

—*Anonymous*

~***~

Hinduism, an inclusive religion: Hinduism is in the first place a non-dogmatic inclusive religion and would have taken even Islam and Christianity into itself, if they had tolerated the process.

—*Aurobindo Ghosh*

~***~

His will: We cannot know in any given situation what God's will is until we become spiritually illumined. Throughout the ages, there have been a few rare souls, who live in a state of union with God.

—*Swami Prabhavananda*

~***~

Homeland: A person who truly feels: 'The world is my homeland; it is my America, my India, my Philippines, my England, my Africa', will never lack scope for a useful and happy life. His natural local pride will know limitless expansion; he will be in touch with creative universal currents.

—Paramahansa Yogananda

~***~

Honest disagreement: Honest disagreement is often a good sign of progress.

—Mahatma Gandhi

~***~

Honesty: A person should not be too honest. Straight trees are cut first and honest people are screwed first.

—Chanakya

~***~

Honoured friends: Be ye as if all men are your close kin and honoured friends.

—Baha'u'llah

~***~

Hope: I find hope in the darkest of days, and focus in the brightest. I do not judge the universe.

—Dalai Lama

~***~

Human form: The last desire to be God in human form, to be one with him.

—Lal Ded

~***~

Human life: Poems are the result of peak happiness or sorrow. Common traits of both happiness and sorrow are tears. In one case, tears will be sweet. In another case, they will be salty. Human life is combination of both.

—A.P.J. Abdul Kalam

~***~

Humanity: Be breath of life to the body of humankind,

dew to the soil of the human heart, and a fruit upon the tree of humanity.

—Baha'u'llah

~***~

Humanity: You must not lose faith in humanity. Humanity is an ocean; if a few drops of the ocean are dirty, the ocean does not become dirty.

—Mahatma Gandhi

~***~

Humans: God never punishes you. He has never lost hope on the human beings.

—Sri Sri Ravishankar

~***~

Humble: Be humble more than a blade of grass, more tolerant than a tree, offering respect on to others and never expecting any in return.

—Chaitanya Mahaprabhu

~***~

Humble: If you are wealthy, be humble. Plants bend when they bear fruit.

—Shirdi Sai Baba

~***~

Humility: If you are humble, nothing will touch you, neither praise nor disgrace, because you know what you are.

—Mother Teresa

~***~

Humility: We come nearest to the great when we are great in humility.

—Rabindranath Tagore

~***~

Hunger: There is a terrible hunger for love.

—Mother Teresa

~***~

Hurt and love: Hurt is part of love. You can get hurt only when you love; otherwise—impossible.

—Sri Sri Ravishankar

❑

I

"I": Of what material is the 'I' made; how difficult it is to look into its nature. We cannot forget the idea, though it is nothing but ourself.

—*Sant Tukaram*

~***~

I: I, the ocean of mind, drink all creation's waves.
Eternity and I, one united ray.
I, a tiny bubble of laughter,
Have become the Sea of Mirth Itself.

—*Paramahansa Yogananda*

~***~

I" concept: When the 'I' concept perishes, the body-sense will necessarily perish like a great tree, whose roots are sawn off.

—*Yoga Vashisht*

~***~

Idea: Take up one idea. Make that one idea your life—think of it, dream of it, live on that idea. Let the brain, muscles, nerves, every part of your body, be full of that idea, and just leave every other idea alone.

—*Swami Vivekananda*

~***~

Idea: Many persons have a wrong idea of what

constitutes true happiness. It is not attained through self-gratification but through fidelity to a worthy purpose.

—Addison, Joseph

~✻✻✻~

Ideal: The ultimate goal of a Hindu, a Christian, a Buddhist, a Jew, a Muslim, or a Zoroastrian is the attainment of perfection in Godhead. The ideal is the same whether you call it the beatific vision, illumination *samadhi*, or *nirvana*.

—Swami Prabhavananda

~✻✻✻~

Ideal of perfection: Cherish the ideal of perfection, and to that, relate all your work and all your movements. Though you love the material things of earth, they will not hurt you and you will bring heaven to earth and soul into things.

—Rabindranath Tagore

~✻✻✻~

Ideas: Most sophisticated ideas start with a simple scribble.

—A.P.J. Abdul Kalam

~✻✻✻~

Ignorance: Ignorance is the most important cause of sorrow.

—Sathya Sai Baba

~✻✻✻~

Ignorance: Where ignorance is our master, there is no possibility of a real peace.

—Dalai Lama

~✻✻✻~

Ignorance, selfishness: I believe all suffering is caused by ignorance. People inflict pain on others in the selfish pursuit of their happiness or satisfaction. Yet true happiness comes from a sense of peace and contentment, which, in turn, must be achieved through the cultivation of altruism, of love and compassion, and elimination of ignorance, selfishness, and greed.

—Dalai Lama

~***~

Ignorant: I am ignorant, and I do not know how to swim. O my Beloved Father, please give me Your arm.

—Sant Namdev

~***~

Ignorant and unreal: Unperceived in deep sleep but perceived (in waking and dreams) by those who are ignorant, the whole of this universe is an outcome of ignorance and, therefore, unreal.

—Adi Shankaracharya

~***~

Infinite truth: In our desire for eternal life, we pray for an eternity of our habit and comfort, forgetting that immortality is in repeatedly transcending the definite forms of life in order to pursue the infinite truth of life.

—Rabindranath Tagore

~***~

Illumined souls: Why do we see only a few illumined souls? Because only very few desire and seek that illumination. What trouble we go through in order to pass a college examination or even just to buy a hat! But we don't bring that interest when it comes to praying and meditating.

—Swami Prabhavananda

~***~

Illusion: Reality has no method. Illusion has many methods, many problems and many concepts.

—Ranjit Maharaj

~***~

Immortal spirit: The more you think of yourself as shining immortal spirit, the more eager you will be to be absolutely free of matter, body and senses. This is the intense desire to be free.

—Swami Vivekananda

~***~

Immortality: Immortality is the fruit of sacrifice.

—*Sathya Sai Baba*

~***~

Immortality: Let us not pray to be sheltered from dangers but to be fearless when facing them.

—*Rabindranath Tagore*

~***~

Important page: What would you like to be remembered for? You have to evolve yourself and shape your life. You should write it on a page and that may be a very important page in the book of human history.

—*A.P.J. Abdul Kalam*

~***~

Impurities: Let a wise man remove his impurities, one by one, little by little, day by day, as a smith removes the impurities of silver.

—*Dhammapada*

~***~

In His name: It is not God that is worshipped but the group or authority that claims to speak in His name. Sin becomes disobedience to authority, not violation of integrity.

—*Dr. S. Radhakrishnan*

~***~

In surrender: In surrender, you realize that, 'It is not possible for me to handle my mind or head with all its guilt and with all its rubbish.' Now you say, 'Divine, you take care of this'.

—*Sri Sri Ravishankar*

~***~

In you: More important than what is behind you and what is ahead of you is what is in you. Seek it. Centre in it, act and live.

—*Swami Chinmayananda*

~***~

In your nature: It is your nature to crave the revelation of That which is, for the Eternal, for Truth, for limitless Knowledge. This is why you do not feel satisfied with the evanescent, the untrue, with ignorance and limitation. Your true nature is to yearn for the revelation of what you ARE.

—Anandmayi Ma

~***~

Indian Constitution: I feel that the Constitution is workable; it is flexible and it is strong enough to hold the country together both in peace time and in war time. Indeed, if I may say so, if things go wrong under the new Constitution the reason will not be that we had a bad Constitution. What we will have to say is that Man was vile.

—B.R. Ambedkar

~***~

Indians: We are Indians, firstly and lastly.

—B.R. Ambedkar

~***~

Individual: The tendency in modern civilization is to make the world uniform.... Let the mind be universal. The individual should not be sacrificed.

—Rabindranath Tagore

~***~

Infinity: The Infinity longs for you as much as you long for It.

—Sri Sri Ravishankar

~***~

Inner Eye: When you see with your inner eye, then you realize that you are God and not different from Him.

—Shirdi Sai Baba

~***~

Inner thoughts: As a man thinks in his heart, so is he.

—Proverbs 23:7

~***~

Innovation: It is through the process of innovation that knowledge is converted into wealth. Innovation is capital. Innovation is the key for non-linear growth.

—A.P.J. Abdul Kalam

~***~

Inquire into the Self: Having given up desire, anger, greed and delusion, inquire into the Self—"Who am I?" Being without Self-knowledge and the prisoners of hell, the deluded are tormented.

—Adi Shankaracharya

~***~

Inside that: Dying and giving birth go on inside the One consciousness. But most people misunderstand the pure playoff creative energy. How inside That those are one event.

—Lal Ded

~***~

Inspiration: No great genius could ever draw real inspiration from anywhere except from living Nature.

—Swami Ṛam Tirath

~***~

Instinctive tendencies: Action is no less necessary than thought to the instinctive tendencies of the human frame.

—Mahatma Gandhi

~***~

Institutions: Institutions can create value, add wealth and develop great human resources.

—A.P.J. Abdul Kalam

~***~

Instruments: The power is with the silent ones, who only live and love and then withdraw their personality. They never say 'me' and 'mine'; they are only blessed in being instruments.

—Swami Vivekananda

~***~

Intelligent living: Silently hear everyone. Accept what is good. Reject and forget what is not. This is intelligent living.

—Swami Chinmayananda

~***~

Intelligent Self: The intelligent Self is neither born nor does It die. It did not originate from anything, nor did anything originate from It. It is birthless, eternal, undecaying, and ancient. It is not injured even when the body is killed.

—Katha Upanishad

~****~

Inner Self: That person, who is of the measure of a thumb, is the inner Self dwelling in the hearts of men, limited by the heart, the understanding and the mind. Those who know this become immortal.

—Svetasvatara Upanishad

~****~

Intention of retaliation: 'He reviled me, he beat me and conquered and then plundered me', who express such thoughts, tie their mind with the intention of retaliation. In them, hatred will not cease.

—Dhammapada

~****~

Intentions: Before the throne of the Almighty, man will be judged not by his acts but by his intentions. For God alone reads our hearts.

—Mahatma Gandhi

~****~

Interconnected: Everything is interconnected. My interest is linked to everyone else's. Our survival and future are linked. Therefore, the destruction of your so-called enemy is actually the destruction of yourself.

—Dalai Lama

~****~

Interpretation: If you need a mediator, an interpreter, then you are not seeking truth; what you want is comfort, gratification, and you might just as well take a pill.

—J. Krishnamurthy

~****~

Interpretation of scriptures: The interpretation of the

true scriptures should only be heard from the *Satpurush*. One who understands the nature of God on the basis of the four scriptures, namely: *Samkhya, Yoga, Vedanta* and *Panchratra is the accomplished Jnani* (wise).

—Swaminarayan

~***~

Inter-relations: We can make truth ours by actively modulating its inter-relations. This is the work of art; for reality is not based in the substance of things but in the principle of relationship.

—Rabindranath Tagore

~***~

Intolerance: Intolerance has been the greatest enemy of our progress.

—Dr. S. Radhakrishnan

~***~

Intuitive experience: The true basis of religion is not belief, but intuitive experience. Intuition is the soul's power of knowing God. To know what religion is really all about, one must know God.

—Paramahansa Yogananda

~***~

Iron: Iron sharpeth iron.

—Proverbs

~***~

Island: Be wise. Make for yourself an island. Strive quickly. Purged of stains and sinless you will be ready for heaven, the world of the elect.

—Dhammapada

❑

J

Jealousy: You are not jealous about someone very dear to you. When someone very close to you is very happy, it doesn't bother you, it doesn't bring jealousy in you. When you think so-and-so is very happy and they are not connected to you totally, then the jealousy comes.

—Sri Sri Ravishankar

~***~

Jesus: 'Jesus is born to a virgin' means that Jesus, or the Lord, is born to this virgin area deep inside you which is untouched by any events that are happening in life.

—Sri Sri Ravishankar

~***~

Jesus in disguise: The dying, the cripple, the mental,
the unwanted, the unloved
they are Jesus in disguise.

—Mother Teresa

~***~

Joy: When we rejoice in our fullness, then we can part with our fruits with joy.

—Rabindranath Tagore

~***~

Judging: Judge not according to the appearance, but judge righteous judgment.

—John

❑

K

Key: Don't put the key to your happiness in someone else's pocket.

—Swami Chinmayananda

~***~

Kind: To every human being must ye be infinitely kind.

—Abdu'l-Baha

~***~

Kind traits: Have constructive thoughts, consoling words, compassionate acts.

—Sathya Sai Baba

~***~

Kindness: Real kindness seeks no return.

—Thirukkural

~***~

Kindness: Speak tenderly to them. Let there be kindness in your face, in your eyes, in your smile, in the warmth of your greeting. Always have a cheerful smile. Don't only give your care, but give your heart as well.

—Mother Teresa

~***~

Kindness and compassion: Whether one believes in a religion or not, and whether one believes in rebirth or not, there isn't anyone who doesn't appreciate kindness and compassion.

—Dalai Lama

~***~

Kingdom, peace: If you want a kingdom and get it, you'll have no peace. If you give it away, still you won't be content. Only a soul free of desire can taste eternity. Be living, yet dead! Then knowing comes to live in you.

—Lal Ded

~***~

Know: Know what to Do. Do it Youself.

—Swami Chinmayananda

~***~

Knowing God: Only he who has known God intimately, who lives in His consciousness all the time, can do His will, because his will has become merged in the divine will. Throughout the ages, there have been a few rare souls who live in such a state of union with God.

—Swami Prabhavananda

~***~

Knowing Vedic sentences: The learned know the Vedas to be one continuous whole, the only purpose of which is to demonstrate one thing, viz. knowledge inasmuch as the oneness of the Self is to be known by the understanding of the Vedic sentences.

—Adi Shankaracharya

~***~

Knowledge: First mental understanding is required and after that comes a practical understanding. Intellectual talent is the greatest thing. Without the intellect, one cannot understand. So, you have to understand with the full intellect and then, that knowledge, or that understanding will submerge, because knowledge is a thought.

—Ranjit Maharaj

~***~

Knowledge: It is said in the Sruti (Vedas) that the consciousness of the oneness (of the individual Self and Brahman) is Knowledge, and that of a difference (between them) is Ignorance. Knowledge is, therefore, demonstrated in the Scriptures with great care.

—***Adi Shankaracharya***

~✻✻✻~

Knowledge: Knowledge makes you free from the chains of ignorance, and revives your heart, knowledge takes you out from the darkness of suspicions and superstitions, and gives a new light to your eyes.

—***Hazrat Abu Ali Saqfi***

~✻✻✻~

Knowledge: Learning gives creativity; creativity leads to thinking; thinking provides knowledge; knowledge makes you great.

—***A.P.J. Abdul Kalam***

~✻✻✻~

Knowledge: Man is the only creature engaged in the pursuit and advancement of knowledge on this planet, perhaps in the known universe. Knowing is the fundamental characteristic of every moment of our experience. Our sensation is knowledge of sensation; our emotion is knowledge of emotion. Our seeing is knowledge; our hearing is knowledge; our thinking about the past, present and future is knowledge. Our questioning is knowledge. Our sense that we don't know something is knowledge. Every experience is knowledge. Knowledge is the very fabric of experience.

—***A.P.J. Abdul Kalam***

~✻✻✻~

Knowledge: There are two ways of recognizing how to value and appreciate, ilm, (1) Become a seeker of knowledge (taalibe ilm). (2) Do not restrict this knowledge to knowing only.

—Mufti Mohammed Shafi

~✻✻✻~

Knowledge: Without devotion, knowledge is tasteless. Without knowledge, devotion is mere empty idol worship.

—Swami Chinmayananda

~✻✻✻~

Knowledge: Knowledge without action is useless and irrelevant. Knowledge with action brings prosperity.

—A.P.J. Abdul Kalam

~✻✻✻~

Knowledge and ignorance: The conception (of the existence) of the non-Self is what is called ignorance, the destruction of which is known to be liberation. This destruction is possible by means of Knowledge only, which is incompatible with Ignorance. Actions (compatible with Ignorance) cannot destroy it.

—Adi Shankaracharya

~✻✻✻~

Knowledge, true: He who forsakes lust, hatred and folly is possessed of true knowledge and a serene mind, craves nought of this world or of any other, applies to himself the teachings of the Sacred texts he recites, even though a few in number—such a one shares in the blessings of the Good Life.

—Dhammapada

□

L

Lamp: Light a lamp in the life of someone.

—A.P.J. Abdul Kalam

~***~

Lamp: Be lamp uno those who walk in darkness, and a home to the strangers.

—Baha'u'llah

~***~

Language: A language is as sweet as the tongues of the speakers.

—Sathya Sai Baba

~***~

Languages: All great languages undergo change. Those languages which resist the spirit of change are doomed and will never produce great harvests of thought and literature.

—Rabindranath Tagore

~***~

Laugh: If an enlightened person walks around, do you know how he feels? He feels like taking a stick and beating everybody and asking them to laugh! All has been provided to you, and God is with you every moment. Now, why don't you smile, laugh, and be happy in life!

—Sri Sri Ravishankar

~***~

Law of prophets: Therefore, all things whatsoever ye would that men should do to you, do ye even so to them: for this is the law and the prophets.

—***Golden Rule, Matthew***

~***~

Law, eternal: In this world never is enmity appeased by hatred; enmity is ever appeased by Love. This is the Law Eternal.

—***Dhammapada***

~***~

Leaders: For success in all missions, we need creative leaders, for he can see far into the future.

—***Anonymous***

~***~

Learn: Learn from others' experiences. Use your mind. Remember. Observe. You are not different from others. Most of their experiences are valid for you too.

—***Nisargadatta Maharaj***

~***~

Learning: Go to the ant, thou sluggard; consider her ways, and be wise.

—***Proverbs***

~***~

Learning: The child learns so easily because he has a natural gift, but adults, because they are tyrants, ignore natural gifts and say that children must learn through the same process that they learned by.

—***Rabindranath Tagore***

~***~

Learning: What has learning profited a man, if it has not led him to worship the Good Feet of Him, who is pure knowledge itself?

—***Thirukkural***

~***~

Leela: God is without form, without quality as well as

with form and quality. Watch and see with what endless variety of beautiful forms He plays the play of his *maya* with Himself alone. The *lila* of the all-pervading One goes on and on in this way in infinite diversity. He is without beginning and without end. He is the whole and also the part. The whole and part together make up real Perfection.

—Sri Anandmayi Ma

~***~

Lesson: The most important lesson that man can learn from his life is not that there is pain in this world, but that it depends upon him to turn it into good account, that it is possible for him to transmute it into joy.

—Rabindranath Tagore

~***~

Levels: Beauty has three levels: indication, expression, and exposure. Spirituality indicates, art expresses, and science exposes.

—Sri Sri Ravishankar

~***~

Liberation: Exhaustion of *vasanas* and destruction of mind; both are the same. That is Liberation.

—Amritanandmayi Ma

~***~

Liberation from transmigration: Being devoted completely to the lotus-feet of the Guru, be liberated from transmigration without delay! Thus, by controlling the mind and the senses, you will see the Divine who is dwelling in your heart.

—Adi Shankaracharya

~***~

Liberty: Liberty is a great celestial Goddess, strong, beneficent, and austere, and she can never descend upon a nation by the shouting of crowds, nor by arguments of unbridled passion, nor by the hatred of class against class.

—Annie Besant

~***~

Liberty, social: So long as you do not achieve social liberty, whatever freedom is provided by the law is of no avail to you.

—B.R. Ambedkar

~***~

Life: Life is given to us, we earn it by giving it.

—Rabindranath Tagore

~***~

Life: Life should be great rather than long.

—B.R. Ambedkar

~***~

Life: We believe that mere movement is life, and that the more velocity it has, the more it expresses vitality.

—Rabindranath Tagore

~***~

Life, hard: Hard is the life to live for one who is modest, who always seeks for what is pure, who is disinterested, unassuming, chaste and has insight.

—Dhammapada

~***~

Life, ordinary way of: You must not let your life run in the ordinary way; do something that nobody else has done, something that will dazzle the world. Show that God's creative principle works in you.

—Sant Yogananda

~***~

Life's aim: Make God the Center of your life. Walk the Path of Love. Serve mankind, and, thus, see God in all.

—Sant Tukaram

~***~

Life's purpose: The purpose of our lives is to be happy.

—Dalai Lama

~***~

Light and darkness: Darkness and light go together. A light goes off and darkness is there, and if you turn on the light, darkness automatically goes away. They are one. In the same way, knowledge and ignorance are both one.

Knowledge is the greatest ignorance. More a discerning mind knows, the more ignorant he feels, the more he wants to know!

—*Ramakrishna Paramahansa*

~***~

Light: There is no light without shadows".

—*L.A. Fontain*

~***~

Likes and dislikes: He who has no likes or dislikes towards pleasant and unpleasant objects, but goes about like one asleep, is said to be a liberated person.

—*Yoga Vashisht*

~***~

Lingam: A devotee, who worships the *lingam* or the yoni, is thinking of the fatherhood or motherhood of the universe, the source of creation, preservation, and dissolution.

—*Swami Prabhavananda*

~***~

Literature: Literature elevates the mind.

—*A.P.J. Abdul Kalam*

~***~

Little narrow paths: Come out into the broad light of the day, come out from the little narrow paths, for how can the infinite soul be content to live and die in small ruts?

—*Swami Vivekananda*

~***~

Live: Live not as though there were a thousand years ahead of you. Fate is at your elbow; make yourself good while life and power are still yours.

—*Marcus Aurelius*

~***~

Living and existence: Everybody exists. It is only the few who live. To live, you should have an ideal.

—*Swami Chinmayananda*

~***~

Living life nobly: Never forget that life can only be

nobly inspired and rightly lived if you take it bravely and gallantly, as a splendid adventure in which you are setting out into an unknown country, to face many a danger, to meet many a joy, to find many a comrade, to win and lose many a battle.

—Annie Besant

~***~

Living: Living is not this tawdry, mediocre, disciplined thing which we call our existence. Living is something entirely different; it is abundantly rich, timelessly changing, and as long as we don't understand that eternal movement, our lives are bound to have very little meaning.

—Jiddu Krishnamurti

~***~

Long faces and religion: We must be bright and cheerful. Long faces do not make religion. Religion should be the most joyful thing in the world, because it is the best.

—Swami Vivekananda

~***~

Longing: Longing, the pain of separation, increases the love in you. That increases the prayerfulness in you.

—Sri Sri Ravishankar

~***~

Looking back: Do not look back upon what has been done. Go ahead!

—Swami Vivekananda

~***~

Lord Krishna: The Supreme Lord Krishna's primary purpose for descending and incarnating is relieve the world of any demoniac and negative, undesirable influences that are opposed to spiritual development, yet simultaneously it is His incomparable intention to be perpetually within reach of all humanity.

—Ramanuja

~***~

Lord's name: As clouds are blown away by the wind,

the thirst for material pleasures will be driven away by the utterance of the Lord's name.

—Sri Sarada Devi

~***~

Lord's name: Without the Name of the Lord, all ostentatious displays are useless.

—Sant Ravidas

~***~

Loser: You are no loser until you quit trying.

—Emerson

~***~

Loss and gain: Loss that is gain and death that is life of immortal glory are attained only by the wise.

—Thirukkural

~***~

Love: Love does not claim possession, but gives freedom.

—Rabindranath Tagore

~***~

Love: Love is now and here.

—Sri Sri Ravishankar

~***~

Love: The end of education is character. The end of knowledge is LOVE. LOVE is the scarcest article today.

—Sathya Sai Baba

~***~

Love: Love is the song of the soul, singing to God.

—Anonymous

~***~

Love a mystery: Love is an endless mystery, for it has nothing else to explain it.

—Rabindranath Tagore

~***~

Love and kindness: Love and kindness are the very basis of society. If we lose these feelings, society will face tremendous difficulties; the survival of humanity will be endangered.

—Dalai Lama

~***~

Love in giving: It is not how much we do, but how much love we put in the doing. It is not how much we give, but how much love we put in the giving.

—Mother Teresa

~***~

Loving Krishna: Nobody can love Krishna or establish a relationship with him immediately; but think of him and go on thinking. Then you begin to realize what perfection means, what love means. It is an experimental process.

—Swami Prabhavananda

□

M

Magnet, needle: When the magnet does not attract the needle, the fault lies in the dirt that covers up the needle.

—Sathya Sai Baba

~***~

Majestic and actionless: Subtler than the subtlest, greatest than the greatest, the Self is hidden in the heart of the creature. By the grace of the Lord, the one who is freed from sorrow, sees him who is actionless and majestic.

—Svetasvatara Upanishad

~***~

Make your own future: Stand up, be bold and be strong. Take the whole responsibility on your shoulders and know that you are the creator of your own destiny. All the strength and succour you want is within you. Therefore, make your own future.

—Swami Vivekananda

~***~

Man: Man is the roof and crown of creation. He may be tossed about by uncertain storms of life, but the solution to it lies in his own efforts in finding an ideal, and then raising his personality, from the level of petty emotions, to the loftier heights of the chosen ideal.

—Swami Chinmayananda

~***~

Man: The fish in the water is silent, the animal on the earth is noisy, the bird in the air is singing. But man has in him the silence of the sea, the noise of the earth and the music of the air.

—Rabindranath Tagore

~***~

Man's abiding happiness: Man's abiding happiness is not in getting anything but in giving himself up to what is greater than himself, to ideas which are larger than his individual life, the idea of his country, of humanity, of God.

—Rabindranath Tagore

~***~

Man's freedom: Man's freedom is never in being saved troubles, but it is the freedom to take trouble for his own good, to make the trouble an element in his joy.

—Rabindranath Tagore

~***~

Man's life, independent: Unlike a drop of water which loses its identity when it joins the ocean, man does not lose his being in the society in which he lives. Man's life is independent. He is born not for the development of the society alone, but for the development of his self.

—B.R. Ambedkar

~***~

Manners: Verily, a man teaching his child manners is better than giving one bushel of grain in alms.

—Hazrat Mohammad

~***~

Marriage: What is marriage? Falling in love anew everyday always with the same person.

—Dada J.P. Vaswani

~***~

Master: See the world from the eyes of the Master. This is a sign that you have come to the Master.

—Sri Sri Ravishankar

~***~

Master's grace: Keep the Master's grace in your thoughts, and reflect on his pure teachings.

—***Sant Dadu Dayal***

~***~

Maya: Since it is stated in the *Vedas*, 'There is no diversity here', 'The Lord on account of *Maya* (illusion) is perceived as manifold', and 'The Self, without being born, appears to be born in various ways', it follows that He is born on account of *Maya* alone.

—***Katha Upanishad***

~***~

Meaningful: Old friends pass away, new friends appear. It is just like the days. An old day passes, a new day arrives. The important thing is to make it meaningful: a meaningful friend—or a meaningful day.

—***Dalai Lama***

~***~

Meat eating: One person can eat meat and become absorbed in God, and another can eat vegetables and be a rogue. If you consider vegetarianism from the standpoint of non-killing, remember that even potatoes have life. So, I would say, eat what agrees with you and what you can digest.

—***Swami Prabhavananda***

~***~

Mechanism of confusion: The very examination of the mechanism of confusion shows the way. After all, your confusion is only in your mind, which never rebelled so far against confusion and never got to grips with it. It rebelled only against pain.

—***Nisargadatta Maharaj***

~***~

Medicine of the body politic: Law and order are the medicine of the body politic and when the body politic gets sick, medicine must be administered.

—***B.R. Ambedkar***

~***~

Meditate: Enlighten your desires. Meditate on who are you, quit imagining. What you want is profoundly expensive and difficult to find, yet closeby. Don't search for it. It is nothing, and a nothing within nothing.

—Anonymous

~***~

Meditation: Meditation will help you to find your bonds, loosen them, untie them and cast your moorings.

—Nisargadatta Maharaj

~***~

Meditation: We can all learn to conquer hatred through love by drawing on the power released through the practice of meditation to throw all our weight, all our energy, and all our will on the side of what is patient, forgiving, and selfless in ourselves and others.

—Eknath Easwaran

~***~

Meditation, His presence: Meditation is not just sitting with our eyes closed. We should take every action as worship. We should be able to experience His presence everywhere.

—Mata Amritanandamayi

~***~

Men of achievement: The real men of achievement are people who have the heroism to fuel more and more enthusiasm in their work, when they face more and more difficulties.

—Swami Chinmayananda

~***~

Men, ideas: Men are mortal. So are ideas. An idea needs propagation as much as a plant needs watering. Otherwise, both will wither and die.

—B.R. Ambedkar

~***~

Men, Man: Men are cruel, but Man is kind.

—Rabindranath Tagore

~***~

Merger: As the rivers flowing east and west merge in the sea and become one with it, forgetting they were ever separate rivers, so do all creatures lose their separateness when they merge at last into pure Being.

—Upanishad

~***~

Message: I believe that Bengal has a message for the world. Keshub Chunder Sen delivered that message. Again and again that message has been delivered on the banks of the Ganga, and again and again will that message be delivered and re-delivered in a fuller and yet fuller manner till we listen, till the world listens.

—Chittaranjan Das

~***~

Message of Gita: The message of the Gita is to be found in the second chapter of the Gita where Lord Krishna speaks of the balanced state of mind, of mental equipoise.

—Mahatma Gandhi

~***~

Mighty: He that is slow to anger is better than the mighty; and he that ruleth his spirit than he that taketh a city.

—Proverbs

~***~

Mill's dogma: Every man, who repeats the dogma of Mill that one country is no fit to rule another country, must admit that one class is not fit to rule another class.

—B.R. Ambedkar

~***~

Mind: A mind all logic is like a knife all blade. It makes the hand bleed that uses it.

—Rabindranath Tagore

~***~

Mind: Little by little, through patience and repeated effort, the mind will become stilled in the Self.

—Bhagavad Gita

~***~

Mind: Mind can make a hell of heaven. Or a heaven of hell.

—Swami Chinmayananda

~✻✻✻~

Mind: The mind acts like an enemy for those who do not control it.

—Bhagavad Gita

~✻✻✻~

Mind: The mind is a nervous thief, the mind is a pure cheat. The ruin of sages, men and gods, the mind has a hundred thousand gates.

—Sant Kabir

~✻✻✻~

Mind: The mind is an ocean. It contains so many worlds within itself, mysterious and dimly seen.

—A.P.J. Abdul Kalam

~✻✻✻~

Mind: The mind is the only hurdle which keeps you away from you. The mind says, It is true. Tell the mind, It is not true. Understand the mind, and then it doesn't remain.

—Ranjit Maharaj

~✻✻✻~

Mind: When this mind is causing so much disappointment to you, why don't you drop it! Why do you hang onto that mind.

—Sri Sri Ravishankar

~✻✻✻~

Mind, heart and soul: Whatever you do, devote your whole mind, heart and soul to it.

—Emerson

~✻✻✻~

Mind, simple: It is a great art to have an abundance of knowledge and experience—to know the richness of life, the beauty of existence, the struggles, the miseries, the laughter, the tears—and yet keep your mind very simple; and you can have a simple mind only when you know how to love.

—J. Krishnamurthy

~***~

Mind, tamed: Thinking is difficult to discipline. Mind is flighty, alighting where it listeth. Good is to tame it. The tamed mind is the bearer of happiness.

—Dhammapada

~***~

Mind's tricks: The mind plays so many tricks. The mind is charmed always by a distance. We are not charmed by God because he is very close to us; he is the nearest. So, the mind tries to keep God at a very great distance.

—Sri Sri Ravishankar

~***~

Mind's work: Wear just enough clothes to keep warm. Eat only enough to stop the hunger-pang. As for your mind, let it work to recognize who you are.

—Lal Ded

~***~

Mind, wrongly directed: Whatever an enemy may do to an enemy, whatever a hater may do to a hater, a wrongly directed mind will do to us greater harm.

—Dhammapada

~***~

Mine, not thine: Mine, not thine; this sense of greed is the root of all evil. This distinction is applied even to GOD!—my GOD, not yours! Your GOD, not mine!

—Sathya Sai Baba

~***~

Miserable: Why should a man be miserable even here in the reign of a just and merciful God?

—Swami Vivekananda

~***~

Misery: Behind every misery, there is a hope. The fuel for miserable people is hope. Foreseeing happiness some time in the future, makes one miserable right now. Having desire for some pleasure in the future, either in the world or in heaven, one misses the boat.

—Sri Sri Ravishankar

~***~

Misery: Misery is truly a gift of God. I believe it is a symbol of His compassion.

—Sarada Devi

~***~

Misinterpreter: When writing about the teachings, can you not state that you are only investigating them? Both you and your readers are going on a voyage of discovery together. It is good to use words like 'perhaps' and 'probably' because they introduce an element of doubt in the mind of the reader. Sir, if you do that, you will not run the risk of becoming a misinterpreter.

—J. Krishnamurthy

~***~

Mission wisdom: To see the one in the many, is the casual vision of knowledge. To see the many in the one, is the mission wisdom.

—Swami Chinmayananda

~***~

Mistakes: We must learn from our mistakes to achieve a better standard of life.

—A.P.J. Abdul Kalam

~***~

Modification: Our creation is the modification of relationship.

—Rabindranath Tagore

~***~

Moksha: The four *Vedas,* eighteen *Puranas* and *Itihas* (*Ramayana* and *Mahabharata*), all proclaim that only God and His *Sadhu* can give *moksha.*

—Swaminarayan

~***~

Moment: Every moment is a moment of creativity; don't waste it.

—A.P.J. Abdul Kalam

~***~

Moments: Never be afraid of the moments—thus sings the voice of the ever-lasting.

—Rabindranath Tagore

~***~

Money, morality: Money comes and goes; morality comes and grows.

—Sathya Sai Baba

~***~

Monks and sants: Traditionally, monks and sants have been regarded as beyond caste. They have often been instrumental in teaching harmony and understanding to the prejudiced and intolerant.

—Swami Prabhavananda

~***~

Monster: Anger is the enemy of non-violence and pride is a monster that swallows it up.

—Mahatma Gandhi

~***~

Moral gymnasium: Thank God for giving you this world as a moral gymnasium to help your development, but never imagine you can help the world.

—Swami Vivekananda

~***~

Mosques and temples: All gods are one. There is no difference between a Hindu and a Muslim. Mosque and temple are the same.

—Shirdi Sai Baba

~***~

Mother: I shan't be able to turn away anybody if he addresses me as Mother. I can't contain myself when one draws near me and calls me Mother.

—Sarada Devi

~***~

Mother: If you honour your mother, the Mother of the Universe will guard you against harm.

—Sathya Sai Baba

~***~

Mother: My son, if a thorn pricks your foot, it hurts me like a spear entering my heart. I am the mother of the wicked, as I am the mother of the virtuous. Whenever you are in distress, just say to yourself, 'I have a mother'.

—Sarada Devi

~***~

Mother-tongue: If there be any one among us anxious to leave a name behind him, and not pass away into oblivion like a brute, let him devote himself to his mother-tongue. That is his legitimate sphere, his proper element.

—Michael Madhusudan Dutt

~***~

Movement: Mere movement is life, and that the more velocity it has, the more it expresses vitality.

—Rabindranath Tagore

~***~

Mud: Covered with mud, I spent the entire day looking for mud. Now, I see what's all over me, and give in to loving it.

—Lal Ded

~***~

Multiplied propagation: An error does not become

truth by reason of multiplied propagation, nor does truth become error because nobody sees it.

—Mahatma Gandhi

~***~

Mundane pleasures: Craving the sense pleasures for fulfilment by enjoying them is akin to pouring water into a fissure which has opened up in the ground and reaches into the depths of the earth. It will never be filled. Similarly, the senses will never be satisfied even with the utmost enjoyment of the sense-objects.

—Swaminarayan

~***~

Music: Music fills the infinite between two souls. This has been muffled by the mist of our daily habits.

—Rabindranath Tagore

~***~

Myself, yourself: Try to treat with equal love all the people with whom you have relations. Thus, the abyss between 'myself'.

—Anonymous

□

N

Nama Jap: Most important of all is the Privilege of being a *Bhakta* and to *nama jap* in life even God is not aware of the power of His Name. How can He be? The lotus cannot smell its own fragrance, only the bee can.

—Sant Tukaram

~***~

Nation: A nation is great because of the way its people think.

—A.P.J. Abdul Kalam

~***~

Nation: A nation that has no bridle on its sensuality, can never thrive or survive.

—Sathya Sai Baba

~***~

Nations: Nations are built over generations.

—A.P.J. Abdul Kalam

~***~

Nationalism: Nationalism is not a mere political programme; nationalism is a religion that has come from God; Nationalism is a creed which you shall have to live... You are the instruments of God to save the light, to save the spirit of India from lasting obscuration and abasement...

—Aurobindo Ghosh

~***~

Nationality: Nationality is respectable only when it is on the defence; when it is waging wars of liberation it is sacred; when those of domination, it is accursed.

—Rabindranath Tagore

~***~

Nation's culture: A nation's culture resides in the hearts and in the soul of its people.

—Mahatma Gandhi

~***~

Nature of the Bliss of God: The blissful *darshan* of *Paramatma,* even in the blink of an eye, is more blessed than all the happiness offered by the seductive sense-objects of millions of universes.

—Swaminarayan

~***~

Nature: Learn from Nature, where everything is hidden, and make your life purposeful and meaningful.

—A.P.J. Abdul Kalam

~***~

Nature: Man is reaping success everyday, and that shows there is a rational connection between him and nature.

—Rabindranath Tagore

~***~

Nature: Nature, the greatest of all teachers, is thwarted at every step by the human teacher, who believes in machine-made lessons rather than life lessons, so that the growth of the child's mind is not only injured, but forcibly spoiled.

—Rabindranath Tagore

~***~

Nature: The faith of each is in accordance with one's own nature.

—Bhagavad Gita

~***~

Nature: Nature is never in a hurry. It operates in terms of millions of years.

—A.P.J. Abdul Kalam

~***~

The Nature of God: He is one and unparalleled.

—Swaminarayan

~***~

Near and far: He who lives in our mind is near, though he may actually be far away; but he who is not in our heart is far, though he may really be nearly.

—Chanakya

~***~

Negative and positive: From a negative standpoint, purity of heart is freedom from lust and greed, freedom from craving for the things of the world. But in its positive aspect, purity means that your heart is filled with divine consciousness.

—Swami Prabhavananda

~***~

New-born child: Do not say, It is morning," and dismiss it with a name of yesterday. See it for the first time as a new-born child that has no name.

—Rabindranath Tagore

~***~

Newer peopie: The newer people, of this modern age, are more eager to amass than to realize.

—Rabindranath Tagore

~***~

Night and day: In the night, we stumble over things and become acutely conscious of their separateness, but the day reveals the unity, which embraces them.

—Rabindranath Tagore

~***~

Nirvana: Health is the greatest of gifts; contentment is the greatest wealth; trust is the best of relationships; *Nirvana* is the highest happiness.

—Dhammapada

~***~

No great things: We can do no great things; only small things with great love.

—Mother Teresa

~***~

No religion: A religion that takes no account of practical affairs and does not help to solve them, is no religion.

—Mahatma Gandhi

~***~

'No': A 'No' uttered from the deepest conviction is better than a 'Yes' merely uttered to please, or worse, to avoid trouble.

—Mahatma Gandhi

~***~

Not in abundance: Whatsoever thy hand findeth to do, do it with thy might.

—Ecclesiastes (ch. IX, v. 10)

~***~

No stars to reach: It is not a disgrace not to reach the stars, but it is a disgrace to have no stars to reach for.

—A.P.J. Abdul Kalam

~***~

No world, no body: For a self-realized being, neither the world with its pairs of opposites exists, nor does the body. If there is no world, there can obviously be no body either.

—Anandmayi Ma

~***~

None is attached: As a child, one keeps on being attached to playing. As a youth, one keeps on being attached to maidens. Growing old, one keeps on being attached to anxiety. To the supreme Brahman, none is attached!

—Adi Shankaracharya

~***~

Nothing: People don't understand that illusion is

nothing. How can it block you? How can nothing block you?

—Ranjit Maharaj

~***~

Nuclear weapons of the mind: Peace is not just the absence of war and conflict; it goes well beyond that. Simply transferring the world's nuclear weapons to a museum will not in itself bring about world peace. The nuclear weapons of the mind must first be eliminated.

—Amritanandamayi Ma

□

O

Object of education: The object of education is to give man the unity of truth.... I believe in a spiritual world—not as anything separate from this world—but as its innermost truth.

—Rabindranath Tagore

~***~

Observe: To observe without evaluating is the highest form of intelligence.

—J. Krishnamurthy

~***~

Offering: Whatever you do, make it an offering to me—the food you eat, the sacrifices you make, the help you give, even your suffering.

—Bhagavad Gita

~***~

Oil and water: Oil and water do not mix; similarly, sex and religion don't mix. Remember that! If you feel lustful, admit your weakness. Don't try to cover the dirty spot with rose petals.

—Swami Prabhavananda

~***~

Old friend: Forsake not an old friend; for the new is not comparable to him: a new friend is as new wine; when it is old, thou shalt drink it with pleasure.

—Ecclesiasticus

~***~

Old-in-vain: A man is not an elder simply because his hair is gray. His age is ripe but he is to be known as Old-in-vain.

—Dhammapada

~***~

Omnipresent: God is not to be spoken of as coming down or going up, since He is everywhere.

—Sathya Sai Baba

~***~

Omnipresent: Its hands and feet are everywhere, its eyes and heads are everywhere, its ears are everywhere. It (Brahman) stands encompassing all in the world.

—Svetasvatara Upanishad

~***~

One: There is some power, someone who is really caring for you—not just someone: there is only One in the whole universe. That One in the Universe is caring and taking care. Relax; just be peaceful.

—Sri Sri Ravishankar

~***~

One: Thou art I, I am Thou, Knowing, Knower, Known, as One!

—Paramahansa Yogananda

~***~

One for all: None should remain satisfied with one's own elevation only, but should incessantly strive for the social uplift of all, realise one's own elevation in the elevation of others.

—Swami Dayanand Saraswati

~***~

Oneness: Everyman ought to be taught that religions are but the varied expressions of the Religion, which is

Oneness, so that each may choose the path that suits him best.

—Swami Vivekananda

~***~

One being, one moment: When you see yourself and someone else as one being, when you know the most joyful day and the most terrible night as one moment, then awareness is alone with its Lord.

—Lal Ded

~***~

Open gate: He who wants to do good, knocks at the gate; he who loves, finds the gate open.

—Rabindranath Tagore

~***~

Opportunity: When opportunity knocks, we are either out or sleeping in.

—Swami Chinmayananda

~***~

Orator: The genuine orator exercises a sort of hypnotism over his audience. I have listened to many orators, Indian, English and American; but Keshub Chunder Sen is easily the greatest of all.

—Swami Vivekananda

~***~

Original source: God is the original source of all that is true knowledge and all that is known by physical sciences.

—Swami Dayanand Saraswati

~***~

Origins of untouchability: The Hindu Civilisation... is a diabolical contrivance to suppress and enslave humanity. Its proper name would be infamy. What else can be said of a civilisation which has produced a mass of people...who are treated as an entity beyond human intercourse and whose mere touch is enough to cause pollution?

—B.R. Ambedkar

~***~

Others' faults: To be angry is to revenge the faults of others on ourselves.

—***Swami Chinmayananda***

~ * * * ~

Our actual enemy: Our actual enemy is not any force exterior to ourselves, but our own crying weaknesses, our cowardice, our selfishness, our hypocrisy, our purblind sentimentalism.

—***Aurobindo Ghosh***

~ * * * ~

Outside circumstances: Each one has to find his peace from within. And peace to be real must be unaffected by outside circumstances.

—***Mahatma Gandhi***

~ * * * ~

Outspoken: To be outspoken is easy when you do not wait to speak the complete truth.

—***Rabindranath Tagore***

~ * * * ~

Overcome: Let a man overcome anger by gentleness; let him overcome evil by good; let him overcome the niggard by liberality; let him overcome the liar by truth.

—***Dhammapada***

□

P

Pain: If you would walk the way of love, never feel hurt nor yield to anger, but accept pain as a part of life.

—Dada J.P. Vaswani

~***~

Pain and suffering: Pain is inevitable. Suffering is optional.

—Dalai Lama

~***~

Panorama: To the person who desires nothing and does not get entangled in desires, the manifold changes of nature are one panorama of beauty and sublimity.

—Swami Vivekananda

~***~

Parting with: If you do not want to part with what you have, do not lie and claim that you have nothing, but decline politely saying that circumstances or your own desires prevent you.

—Shirdi Sai Baba

~***~

Pass away: Remember, 'Even This Shall Pass Away'.

—Swami Chinmayananda

~***~

Past: Nothing that was worthy in the past departs; no

truth or goodness realized by man ever dies, or can die.

—Thomas Carlyle

~***~

Path of wisdom: He who does not rouse himself when it is time to rise and though, young and strong, is full of sloth, whose will and thought are weak, that lazy man will not find the Path of Wisdom.

—Dhammapada

~***~

Patience: Patience is all the strength that man needs.

—Sathya Sai Baba

~***~

Patience: Enduring patience is the highest *tapas*; *Nirvana* is the supreme state—so teach the Buddhas. He who oppresses another is no recluse; he who harms another is no ascetic.

—Dhammapada

~***~

Patience: Patience is the power. Patience and time can transform even a leaf of mulberry tree into silk.

—A.P.J. Abdul Kalam

~***~

Peace forever: He who is subtler than the subtle, who in the midst of chaos has created all things of manifold forms, who alone envelops everything—by knowing Him as the auspicious Lord, one attains peace forever.

—Svetasvatara Upanishad

~***~

Presence of God: Meditate and realize this world is filled with the presence of God.

—Svetasvatara Upanishad

~***~

Peace: There is no fire like lust; no ill like hatred; there is no sorrow like personal existence; there is no peace higher than tranquility.

—Dhammapada

~***~

Peace: We can never obtain peace with the outer world until we make peace with ourselves.

—*Dalai Lama*

~***~

Peace: If they seek peace, then seek you peace. And trust in God for He is the One that heareth and knoweth all things.

—*Quran, 8.61*

~***~

Peace: If you have to maintain peace, you have to be strong.

—*A.P.J. Abdul Kalam*

~***~

Peace: For he is our peace, who hath made both one, and hath broken down the middle wall of partition between us.

—*Ephesians (ch. II, v. 14)*

~***~

Peace, inner: If we have no peace, it is because we have forgotten that we belong to each other.

—*Mother Teresa*

~***~

Problems: Problem gives challenge. Challenge propelled with knowledge and work leads to achievements.

—*A.P.J. Abdul Kalam*

~***~

Perception: Who are you? Who am I? Wherefrom have I come? Who is my mother? Who is my father? Reflect over this, having left aside all the universe which is an essenceless dream perception.

—*Adi Shankaracharya*

~***~

Perfect act: A man, who was completely innocent, offered himself as a sacrifice for the good of others, including his enemies, and became the ransom of the world. It was a perfect act.

—*Mahatma Gandhi*

~***~

Perfection: The potentiality of perfection outweighs actual contradictions.... Existence in itself is here to prove that it cannot be an evil.

—Rabindranath Tagore

~***~

Perishable: Perishable is matter, imperishable and immortal is the Lord. He, the only God, rules over both matter and the soul. By meditating on Him, by uniting with Him and becoming one with Him there is in the end complete cessation of the illusion of the world.

—Svetasvatara Upanishad

~***~

Perseverence: It is the cheerful mind that is persevering. It is the strong mind that hews its way through a thousand difficulties.

—Swami Vivekananda

~***~

Pleasure and pain: Every pleasure, physical or mental, needs an instrument. Both the physical and mental instruments are material, they get tired and worn out. The pleasure they yield is necessarily limited in its intensity and duration. Pain is the background of all your pleasures. You want them because you suffer. On the other hand, the very search for pleasure is the cause of pain. It is a vicious circle.

—Nisargadatta Maharaj

~***~

Poetry: The beauty of poetry is that the creation transcends the poet.

—Mahatma Gandhi

~***~

Poets: We poets set men free from their desires.

—Rabindranath Tagore

~***~

Political and social rights: For a successful revolution, it is not enough that there is discontent. What is required is a profound and thorough conviction of the justice, necessity and importance of political and social rights.

—***B.R. Ambedkar***

~***~

Possessions: Whatever we treasure for ourselves, separates us from others; our possessions are our limitations.

—***Rabindranath Tagore***

~***~

Possible: Asks the Possible of the Impossible, 'Where is your dwelling-place?' 'In the dreams of the Impotent,' comes the answer.

—***Rabindranath Tagore***

~***~

Possible: Be kind whenever possible...it is always possible.

—***Dalai Lama***

~***~

Pot: If there is a pot, a pot is perceived, And if the pot is broken, its brokenness is perceived; If there is no pot at all, Is not its absence perceived as well?

—***Sant Gyaneshwar***

~***~

Potato plant: A man who prides himself on his ancestory is like the potato plant, the best part of which is underground.

—***Dr. S. Radhakrishnan***

~***~

Practice: The purpose of every practice—spiritual practice, meditation, breathing techniques, and *kriya*, all this—is to uncover something that blocks the expression of Divine Love.

—***Sri Sri Ravishankar***

~***~

Practice: Taste goodness before you recommend it. Practice meditation before you preach it. Gain bliss before you offer it to others.

—***Swami Chinmayananda***

~***~

Practice what you preach: He who eats no molasses must not even keep molasses about. If he does, and yet tells others not to eat it, they won't listen to him.

—***Ramakrishna Paramahansa***

~***~

Practice, preaching: An ounce of practice is worth more than tons of preaching.

—***Mahatma Gandhi***

~***~

Praise: Praise shames me, for I secretly beg for it.

—***Rabindranath Tagore***

~***~

Praise: Solid rock is not shaken by the gale. The wise man is not moved by praise or blame.

—***Dhammapada***

~***~

Praise: To God be the praise. I am only the slave of God.

—***Shirdi Sai Baba***

~***~

Praised: There never was, nor will be, nor is there now to be found anyone who stands wholly praised or utterly condemned.

—***Dhammapada***

~***~

Prayer: Prayer is not a practice; it is a happening.

—***Sri Sri Ravishankar***

~***~

Prayer: Prayer simply means a longing of the heart, it is the wish felt—it may be expressed, or not expressed. It may take the form of human language or it may never be uttered at all; still it is a prayer, if God only hears it in the secret recess of the heart.

—***Keshub Chander Sen***

~***~

Preach and practice: Live morality before you talk of it.

—*Anonymous*

~***~

Present moment: We should not fret for what is past, nor should we be anxious about the future; men of discernment deal only with the present moment.

—*Chanakya*

~***~

Present moment: The present moment, making the mind be there—now, now, now—makes you like a child: innocent and still a lot of wisdom and depth.

—*Sri Sri Ravishankar*

~***~

Pretension: Even if a snake is not poisonous, it should pretend to be venomous.

—*Chanakya*

~***~

Price of success: Judge your success by what you had to give up in order to get it.

—*Dr. S. Radhakrishnan*

~***~

Pricks: It is hard for thee to kick against the pricks.

—*Adversity*

~***~

Pride: Your pride in yourself and your wants. These steal your energy along road. If you can kill these robbers and become the servant of everyone, you'll meet the Lord in meditation. And see what you used to protect as just a pile of ashes.

—*Lal Ded*

~***~

Priesthood: Those institutions which are static in their nature raise walls of division; this is why, in the history of religions, priesthood has always maintained dissensions and hindered the freedom of man.

—*Rabindranath Tagore*

~***~

Primary focus: The primary focus of the students should be to excel in their studies.

—***Anonymous***

~***~

Power: Patience and tolerance is power; don't lose it.

—***A.P.J. Abdul Kalam***

~***~

Problem: To solve a problem, you must trace it to its source. Only in the dissolution of the problem in the universal solvents of inquiry and dispassion, can its right solution be found.

—***Nisargadatta Maharaj***

~***~

Problems and aspirations: Every age hath its own problem, and every soul its particular aspiration. The remedy the world needeth in its present-day afflictions can never be the same as that which a subsequent age may require.

—***Abdu'l-Baha***

~***~

Problems: Never let problems rule you.

—***A.P.J. Abdul Kalam***

~***~

Proficiency: Efficiency is the capacity to bring proficiency into expression.

—***Swami Chinmayananda***

~***~

Progress: Progress is activity of today and assurance of tomorrow.

—***Emerson***

~***~

Progress: Shared vision is progress.

—***A.P.J. Abdul Kalam***

~***~

Progress: When learning is purposeful, creativity

blossoms; when creativity blossoms, thinking emanates; when thinking emanates, knowledge is lit; when knowledge is lit, the nation progresses.

—***A.P.J. Abdul Kalam***

~***~

Progress of our soul: The progress of our soul is like a perfect poem. It has an infinite idea which once realised makes all movements full of meaning and joy.

—***Rabindranath Tagore***

~***~

Promises: Fulfill any promises you have made.

—***Shirdi Sai Baba***

~***~

Prosperity: Prosperity is like wine, which goes to the head, and makes man forget his Creator.

—***Swami Chinmayananda***

~***~

Prosperity and adversity: In the day of prosperity, be joyful, but in the day of adversity, consider.

— ***Ecclesiastes***

~***~

Pure playoff: Dying and giving birth go on inside the One consciousness. But most people misunderstand the pure playoff creative energy. How inside That those are one event.

—***Lal Ded***

~***~

Purification: Purify yourself by a well-ordered and useful life. Watch over your thoughts, feelings, words and actions. This will clear your vision.

—***Nisargadatta Maharaj***

~***~

Purity and depression: The moment purity comes, depression cannot be there; it goes away.

—***Sri Sri Ravishankar***

~***~

Purity: From a negative standpoint, purity of heart is freedom from lust and greed, freedom from craving for the things of the world. But in its positive aspect, purity means that your heart is filled with divine consciousness.

—Swami Prabhavananda

~***~

Purity: The power of purity—it is a definite power.

—Swami Vivekananda

~***~

Purpose of life: If the water in your jug,
Is brackish and low.
Smash the jug,
And come to the river.

—A.P.J. Abdul Kalam

~***~

Purposeless activity: Endless, purposeless activity eventually leads to helpless feelings that perpetuate another cycle of more meaningless thoughts and actions.

—A.P.J. Abdul Kalam

❑

Q

Question your dream: When you shall begin to question your dream, awakening will not be far away.

—*Nisargadatta Maharaj*

R

Ram: Ram is my father. Ram is my mother. He gives life to all beings.

—Sant Namdev

~***~

Religion: Religion, like poetry, is not a mere idea, it is expression. The self-expression of God is in the endless variety of creation; and our attitude towards the Infinite Being must also in its expression have a variety of individuality ceaseless and unending. Those sects which jealously build their boundaries with too rigid creeds excluding all spontaneous movement of the living spirit may hoard their theology but they kill religion.

—Rabindranath Tagore

~***~

Rational position: Refusal to believe until proof is given is a rational position; denial of all outside of our own limited experience is absurd.

—Annie Besant

~***~

Raving maniac: But for my faith in God, I should have been a raving maniac.

—Mahatma Gandhi

~***~

Reading: Give one hour a day exclusively for book reading and, in a few years, you will become a knowledge centre.

—A.P.J. Abdul Kalam

~***~

Reading the world: We read the world wrong and say that it deceives us.

—Rabindranath Tagore

~***~

Real master: Servant is the real master. Who becomes a master, is one who serves. God has been serving you day and night. He takes care of everything for you.

—Sri Sri Ravishankar

~***~

Realisation, ignorance: Realisation is but the opposite of ignorance. To take the world as real and one's self as unreal is ignorance, the cause of sorrow. To know the self as the only reality and all else as temporal and transient is freedom, peace and joy. When you can see everything as it is, you will also see yourself as you are. The thought 'I am' is the polishing cloth. Use it.

—Nisargadatta Maharaj

~***~

Reality: Reality is not to be achieved, it is there. After this thorough understanding, nothing is required.

—Ranjit Maharaj

~***~

Reality: When a jar is placed on the ground, we have the ground with a jar; when the jar is taken away, we have the ground without a jar. But when neither of these conditions exists, the ground exists in its unqualified state. It is in this same way that the ultimate Reality exists.

—Sant Gyaneshwar

~***~

Reality of body: Who says the body exists? There is no question at all of name and form. To wonder whether a realized Being sees anything outside of Himself, is also beside the point. Who is there to whom he can say: 'Give to my body'! Yet this state of wanting is precisely the reason for one's belief in the reality of the body.

—*Sri Anandamayi Ma*

~***~

Recreative solitude: There is no companion like solitude. One who knows how to tune himself to the inner silence, even in the midst of the din and roar of the marketplace, enjoys the most recreative solitude.

—*Swami Chinmayananda*

~***~

Redeemer: If I did not commit any sins, O Infinite Lord, how would You have acquired the name, 'Redeemer of sinners'?

—*Sant Ravidas*

~***~

Reformer: Political tyranny is nothing compared to the social tyranny and a reformer, who defies society is a more courageous man than a politician, who defies Government.

—*B.R. Ambedkar*

~***~

Relationships: The relationship between husband and wife should be one of the closest friends.

—*B.R. Ambedkar*

~***~

Relationship, its meaning: Who is your wife? Who is your son? This transmigratory world is very strange! To whom do you belong? Who are you? Whence have you come? Think of what is the Truth, bewildered as you are.

—*Adi Shankaracharya*

~***~

Religion: No religion has mandated killing others as a requirement for its sustenance or promotion.

—*A.P.J. Abdul Kalam*

~***~

Religion: Religion is the truth of our complete being, the consciousness of our personal relationship with the infinite; it is the true center of gravity of our life.

—Rabindranath Tagore

~***~

Religion: Religion must not be considered true because it is necessary, but necessary because it is true.

—Swami Chinmayananda

~***~

Religion and man: It is said a man without religion is like a horse without a bridle.

—Dr. S. Radhakrishnan

~***~

Religion, mine: I do not need any temples; I do not need any complicated philosophy. Our own brain, our own heart is our temple; the philosophy is kindness. This is my simple religion.

—Dalai Lama

~***~

Religion, object of: The true object of religion is to bind mankind together, and to bind them all to God. If we see that in the name of religion, men, instead of promoting peace on earth and goodwill among men, are trying to show their antagonism and animosity towards each other, then certainly we must stand forward with our voice of protest, and say that religion is defeating its own legitimate object.

—Keshub Chander Sen

~***~

Religion, the teacher: I like the religion that teaches liberty, equality and fraternity.

—B.R. Ambedkar

~***~

Remain silent: Better remain silent, better not even think, if you are not prepared to act.

—Annie Besant

~***~

Remaking ourselves: As human beings, our greatness lies not so much in being able to remake the world—that is the myth of the atomic age—as in being able to remake ourselves.

—Mahatma Gandhi

~***~

Remember, observe: Use your mind. Remember. Observe. You are not different from others. Most of their experiences are valid for you too. Think clearly and deeply, go into the structure of your desires and their ramifications. They are a most important part of your mental and emotional make-up and powerfully affect your actions. Remember, you cannot abandon what you do not know. To go beyond yourself, you must know yourself.

—Nisargadatta Maharaj

~***~

Remembering yourself: Remembering yourself is virtue, forgetting yourself is sin.

—Nisargadatta Maharaj

~***~

Removal of desire: Desire can be eradicated from the roots by firmly imbibing the four attributes of: *Jnan, Atmanishtha, Vairagya, Dharma* and the full-fledged devotion to God.

—Swaminarayan

~***~

Renown: Those who live without reproach truly live. Those who live without renown don't live at all.

—Thirukkural

~***~

Repetition: Repeating what we did before for several decades with more of the same may not be the way to proceed further.

—A.P.J. Abdul Kalam

~***~

Responsibility, universal: Today, more than ever

before, life must be characterized by a sense of Universal responsibility, not only nation to nation and human to human, but also human to other forms of life.

—Dalai Lama

~***~

Restless: The mind is restless and difficult to restrain, but it is subdued by practice.

—Bhagavad Gita

~***~

Results of man's actions: God helps by facing man with the results of his actions and demanding that the balance should be restored. *Karma* is the law that works for righteousness; it is the healing hand of God.

—Nisargadatta Maharaj

~***~

Revealing your thoughts: Do not reveal what you have thought upon doing, but by wise council, keep it secret being determined to carry it into execution.

—Chanakya

~***~

Revolutions and ideas: All revolutions consist of the within" fighting against invasion from 'without'.... All great human movements are related to some great idea.

—Rabindranath Tagore

~***~

Revolution, successful: For a successful revolution, it is not enough that there is discontent. What is required, is a profound and thorough conviction of the justice, necessity and importance of political and social rights.

—B.R. Ambedkar

~***~

Right: The Constitution only gives people the right to pursue happiness. You have to catch it yourself.

—Benjamin Franklin

~***~

Right guidance: Right guidance at right time is indeed a great mission.

—Anonymous

~***~

Righteous life: From the emperor down to the common man, the cultivation of the righteous life is the foundation for all.

—A.P.J. Abdul Kalam

~***~

Rights, political and social: For a successful revolution, it is not enough that there is discontent. What is required is a profound and thorough conviction of the justice, necessity and importance of political and social rights.

—B.R. Ambedkar

~***~

Rituals: I do not favour elaborate rituals, displays of asceticism or preoccupation with austerities. Even dogs come in saffron colour and bears have matted fur. If living in caves is being spiritual, then rats, who inhabit caves, must be doing *sadhana* (or spiritual practice).

—Sant Tukaram

~***~

Road: We can look upon a road from two different points of view. One regards it as dividing us from the object of desire.... The other sees it as the road, which leads us to our destination.

—Ranbindranath Tagore

~***~

Rope: You need someone from the other shore to throw the rope, which you can hold on [to] and cross.

—Sri Sri Ravishankar

~***~

Rust: If I rest, I rust.

—Swami Chinmayananda

❑

S

'Shila': Self-discipline, although difficult, and not always easy while combating negative emotions, should be a defensive measure. That is 'shila' or moral ethics. Once we develop this by familiarizing ourselves with it, along with mindfulness and conscientiousness, eventually that pattern and way of life will become a part of our own life.

—Dalai Lama

~***~

Share: Thousands of candles can be lighted from a single candle, and the life of the candle will not be shortened. Happiness never decreases by being shared.

—Buddha

~***~

Safe: Bigotry tries to keep truth safe in its hand with a grip that kills it.

—Rabindranath Tagore

~***~

Saintly person: A saintly person cannot be prevented by any worldly hindrances and compulsions from going to Saints to meet them for *Darshan* or *Satsang* and further says that they are the real Saints and enjoy the fruits of liberation and freedom.

—Sant Kabir

~***~

Saints: Saints like Gandhi, on the other hand, have made not only tangible material sacrifices, but also the more difficult renunciation of selfish motive and private goal, merging their inmost being in the stream of humanity as a whole.

—Paramahansa Yogananda

~***~

Same: All gods are one. There is no difference between a Hindu and a Muslim. Mosque and temple are the same.

—Shirdi Sai Baba

~***~

Samskritam literature: Samskritam literature is national in one sense, but its purpose has been universal. That was why, it commanded the attention of people, who were not followers of a particular culture.

—Dr. S. Radhakrishnan

~***~

Sanatan dharma, life itself: We speak often of the Hindu religion, of the *Sanatan Dharma,* but few of us really know what that religion is. Other religions are preponderatingly religions of faith and profession, but the *Sanatan Dharma* is life itself; it is a thing that has not so much to be believed as lived.

—Aurobindo Ghosh

~***~

Sanatana Dharma: *Sanatana Dharma* has many scriptures: The *Veda,* the *Vedanta,* the *Gita,* the *Upanishads,* the *Darshanas,* the *Puranas,* the *Tantras*...but it's real, the most authoritative scripture is in the heart in which the Eternal has his dwelling.

—Aurobindo Ghosh

~***~

Sanctuary: Chant his name as often as you can. When you think of God, you are in the sanctuary. Nothing can touch you.

—Swami Prabhavananda

~***~

Sandalwoood: Sandalwood perfumes even the axe that hurls it down! The more we rub sandalwood against a stone, the more its fragrance spreads. Burn it, and it wafts its glory through the entire neighbourhood. Such is the enchanting beauty of forgiveness in life.

—Swami Chinmayananda

~***~

Sannyasi: A *sannyasi* must give up 'woman and gold'; he cannot accept it anymore. One must not swallow one's own spittle. When a *sannyasi* gives something to another, he knows that it is not himself who gives. Kindness belongs to God alone. How can a man lay claim to it?

—Ramakrishna Paramahansa

~***~

Sanskrit: Sanskrit language has been universally recognised by those competent to form a judgement and is one of the most magnificent, the most perfect, the most prominent and wonderfully sufficient literary instrument developed by the human mind.

—Aurobindo Ghosh

~***~

Sarva dharma: Let brothers and sisters from one end of the world, speak in all brotherly love, all affection, and one sweetness, to their brothers and sisters in the other extremity of the world. Then we shall succeed in rearing up one vast cathedral in this world, where men of all nations and races shall glorify the Supreme Ruler of the Universe.

—Keshub Chander Sen

~***~

Sadguru: There is none parallel to the *Sadguru*. He is unique in all seven islands, nine segments, three regions and 21 universes. The greatness of the *Sadguru* is above all. The great favour extended by him cannot be received from any other source.

—Sant Kabir

~***~

Satisfactory answers: Keep asking questions till you get satisfactory answers.

—A.P.J. Abdul Kalam

~***~

Satisfy your mind: Give up the thirst for accumulation of wealth. Create in your mind the thought of Reality, without any thirst. What you get, the wealth acquired through your past deeds, with that, satisfy your mind.

—Adi Shankaracharya

~***~

Satsang and Dussaya: *Satsang* that is associating with the good is good. *Dussaya,* or associating with evil-minded people, is evil and must be avoided.

—Shirdi Sai Baba

~***~

Saviours: The saviours of the world do not come to foster inimical doctrinal divisions; their teachings should not be used towards that end. It is something of a misnomer even to refer to the New Testament as the 'Christian' Bible, for it does not belong exclusively to any one sect.

—Paramahansa Yogananda

~***~

School of eternal man: In the light of reincarnation, life changes its aspect, for it becomes the school of the eternal Man within us, who seeks therein his development, the Man that was and is and shall be, for whom the hour will never strike.

—Annie Besant

~***~

Science: Science is life, but it's pursuit is a combination of great elation and great despair.

—A.P.J. Abdul Kalam

~***~

Secret of success: How do you go about finding anything? By keeping your mind and heart on it. Interest there must be and steady remembrance. To remember what needs to be remembered is the secret of success. You come to it through earnestness.

—Nisargadatta Maharaj

~***~

Secret of true life: What is the secret of the true life? To remain still in the midst of activity and to be vibrantly awake while in meditation.

—Dada Sadhu Vaswani

~***~

Seeing the false: Seeing the false as false is meditation. This must go on all the time.

—Nisargadatta Maharaj

~***~

Seek peace: If they seek peace, then you seek peace. And trust in God for He is the One that heareth and knoweth all things.

—Quran

~***~

Seeking happiness: I believe that the very purpose of our life is to seek happiness. That is clear. Whether one believes in religion or not, whether one believes in this religion or that religion, we all are seeking something better in life. So, I think the very motion of our life is towards happiness....

—Dalai Lama

~***~

Seer, seen: The seers, the seen, and the process of seeing all merge. The knowledge, the knower, and the known, they all merge, become one — that is Divine Love.

—Sri Sri Ravishankar

~***~

Seers: The seers of ancient India had, in their experiments and efforts at spiritual training and the conquest of the body, perfected a discovery which in its importance to the future of human knowledge dwarfs the divinations of Newton and Galileo, even the discovery of the inductive and experimental method in Science was not more momentous....

—Aurobindo Ghosh

~***~

Self: When identified with the ego, the Self appears other than what it is. It may appear smaller than a hair's breadth. But know the Self to be infinite.

—Svetasvatara Upanishad

~***~

Self-knowledge: Sever the ignorant doubt in your heart with the sword of self-knowledge. Observe your discipline.

—Bhagavad Gita

~***~

Self or Brahm: All is the Self or Brahman. The saint, the sinner, the lamb, the tiger, even the murderer, as far as they have any reality, can be nothing else, because there is nothing else.

—Swami Vivekananda

~***~

Steadfast: One who has control over the mind is tranquil in heat and cold, in pleasure and pain, and in honour and dishonour; and is ever steadfast with the Supreme Self.

—Bhagavad Gita

~***~

Self-realization: Self-realization is the knowing in all parts of body, mind and soul that you are now in possession of the kingdom of God; that you do not have to pray that it come to you; that God's omnipresence is to your omnipresence; and that all that you need to do is improve your knowing.

—Paramahansa Yogananda

~***~

Sense: Death overpowers the man who is gathering the

flowers of sense, even before he is satiated in his pleasure.

—Dhammapada

~***~

Supreme: The Supreme is the easiest to reach for it is your very being. It is enough to stop thinking and desiring anything, but the Supreme.

—Nisargadatta Maharaj

~***~

Servants of Allah: And the servants of Allah...are those who walked on the earth in humility, and when the ignorant address them, they say 'Peace'....

—Quran

~***~

Serve: Brood less, smile more and serve all.

—Swami Chinmayananda

~***~

Service a joy: I slept and dreamt that life was joy. I awoke and saw that life was service. I acted and behold, service was joy.

—Rabindranath Tagore

~***~

Service, a religious duty: Widen your shriveled heart, make the interests of others your own and serve them as much as you can by sympathy, kindness and presents and so forth. So long as one enjoys the things of this world and has needs and wants, it is necessary to minister to the needs of one's fellow men also. Otherwise one cannot be called a human being. Whenever you have the opportunity, give to the poor, feed the hungry, nurse the sick—do service as a religious duty and you will come to know by direct perception that the person served, the one who serves and the act of service are separate only in appearance.

—Sri Anandamayi Ma

~***~

Sex-distinction: Is there any sex-distinction in the *Atman* (Self)? Out with the differentiation between man and woman—all is *Atman*! Give up the identification with the body and stand up!

—Swami Vivekananda

~***~

Sex energy: The sex energy, if it is not dissipated, plays a great part in religion. When conserved, it becomes transmuted into spiritual energy. Conserving means overcoming lust.

—Swami Prabhavananda

~***~

Shadows: There can't be shadows without light somewhere nearby.

—Emerson

~***~

Sidhi: If you could give yourself, then your needs will all be taken care of, more than it is needed. That is called *sidhi*—whatever is needed comes before it is needed.

—Sri Sri Ravishankar

~***~

Sign of attainment: Meditate and grow humble. Watch anger and wanting will turn to ashes. Study the ground Lalla, as a sign of attainment.

—Lal Ded

~***~

Silence: Silence is the speech of the spiritual seeker.

—Sathya Sai Baba

~***~

Silence: The highest form of grace is silence.

—Swami Chinmayananda

~***~

Silence of the heart: Before you speak, it is necessary for you to listen, for God speaks in the silence of the heart.

—Mother Teresa

~***~

Simple: Be simple. Be sincere.

—*Sathya Sai Baba*

~***~

Sin: It is not God that is worshipped but the group or authority that claims to speak in His name. Sin becomes disobedience to authority, not violation of integrity.

—*Dr. S. Radhakrishnan*

~***~

Sincerity and happiness: Once you start working on something, don't be afraid of failure and don't abandon it. People who work sincerely are the happiest.

—*Chanakya*

~***~

Sloth: Fools and witless persons give themselves to sloth. The wise value vigilance as their best treasure.

—*Dhammapada*

~***~

Small road, broad road: Small minds select narrow roads; expand your mental vision and take to the broad road of helpfulness, compassion and service.

—*Sathya Sai Baba*

~***~

Smile: We must wear the gown of smile and our soul must wear the gown of virtues to protect it.

—*A.P.J. Abdul Kalam*

~***~

Social elevation: We must shape our course ourselves and by ourselves.... Political power cannot be a panacea for the ills of the Depressed Classes. Their salvation lies in their social elevation. They must cleanse their evil habits. They must improve their bad ways of living.... They must be educated.... There is a great necessity to disturb their pathetic contentment and to instill into them that divine discontent which is the spring of all elevation.

—*B.R. Ambedkar*

~***~

Social liberty: So long as you do not achieve social liberty, whatever freedom is provided by the law, is of no avail to you.

—B.R. Ambedkar

~***~

Social reformer: Political tyranny is nothing compared to the social tyranny and a reformer who defies society is a more courageous man than a politician who defies government.

—B.R. Ambedkar

~***~

Son and mother: If my son wallows in the dust or mud, it is I who have to wipe all the dirt off his body and take him to my lap.

—Sarada Devi

~***~

Sons of God: We are Sons of God and must be even as He.

—Aurobindo Ghosh

~***~

Sorrow, the tax: If you just look into all the pleasures or joy that you get in life from the world, from anything—they all come with a tax. You have to pay a tax for them. And this tax is sorrow.

—Sri Sri Ravishankar

~***~

Sorrows and sufferings: Saints are born for liberating other human beings from their sorrows and sufferings through their grace.

—Sant Kabir

~***~

Soul: If a man talks of divine knowledge, while his heart is full of pride in wealth, what pleasure does it yield the soul to serve him?

—Sant Tukaram

~***~

Soul: The progress of our soul is like a perfect poem. It has an infinite idea which once realised makes all movements full of meaning and joy.

—***Rabindranath Tagore***

~***~

Soul: The soul is the locus, the agent, and all the varied content of human experience.

—***A.P.J. Abdul Kalam***

~***~

Soul: With the rising of the sun, the night is brought to its end; with the touch of the Philosopher's Stone, copper is immediately transformed into gold. When one meets the Supreme Philosopher's Stone, the *Guru*, then the soul blends with the Supreme Soul, and the stubborn doors are opened wide.

—***Sant Ravidas***

~***~

Source: You are the source that you are seeking. You are in your driveway, but you are searching for your home.

—***Sri Sri Ravishankar***

~***~

Speech: Most of the sorrow in the world is because of this: speech—what people say. If they kept their lips tight, ninety per cent of the problems in the world would be over.

—***Sri Sri Ravishankar***

~***~

Speech-irritation: Let a man be watchful of speech-irritation. Let him control his speech. Abandoning the sins of speech, let him practise virtue with his speech.

—***Dhammapada***

~***~

Spiritual development: By keeping our mind on God constantly, while engaged in any work, the benefit will reach all members of the family. The ultimate aim in life should not be to amass wealth for children and relatives; it should be to focus on our own spiritual development.

—Amritanandmayi Ma

~***~

Spiritual meaning: The man whose acquaintance with the world does not lead him deeper than science leads him, will never understand what it is that the man with the spiritual vision finds in these natural phenomena.

—Rabindranath Tagore

~***~

Spiritual revolution: We must return and seek the sources of life and strength within ourselves.... It is the spiritual revolution we forsee and the material is only its shadow and reflex.

—Aurobindo Ghosh

~***~

Spiritual sustenance: Human beings are of such nature that they should have not only material facilities but spiritual sustenance as well. Without spiritual sustenance, it is difficult to get and maintain peace of mind.

—Dalai Lama

~***~

Spirituality: Spirituality is neither the privilege of the poor nor the luxury of the rich. It is the choice of the wise man.

—Swami Chinmayananda

~***~

Spirituality: Spirituality is the master key of the Indian mind. It is this dominant inclination of India which gives character to all the expressions of her culture. In fact, they have grown out of her inborn spiritual tendency of which her religion is a natural outflowering.

—Aurobindo Ghosh

~***~

Standing: Have a balance in you. If there is balance, then you can dance, then life becomes a dance. If you can't stand, then you cannot dance, and 'standing' is appreciating, looking at all the values in life and keeping your life in its very center.

—Sri Sri Ravishankar

~***~

Stiffness: In life, any time you become stiff—and there you get a slap! Become soft; smile there. Any stiffness, life just smoothens it out, evens it out, in you.

—Sri Sri Ravishankar

~***~

Straightening crooked thinking: Just as a fletcher makes straight his arrow, the wise man makes straight his crooked thinking. This is difficult to guard. This is hard to restrain.

—Dhammapada

~***~

Stream of life: The same stream of life that runs through my veins night and day runs through the world and dances in rhythmic measures.

—Rabindranath Tagore

~***~

Strength: Climbing to the top demands strength, whether it is to the top of Mount Everest or to the top of your career.

—A.P.J. Abdul Kalam

~***~

Strong mind: A strong mind can defeat problems and succeed.

—A.P.J. Abdul Kalam

~***~

Struggle for freedom: There is to be found in every religion the manifestation of the struggle towards freedom. It is the groundwork of all morality, of unselfishness, which means getting rid of the idea that human beings are the same as this little body.

—Swami Vivekananda

~***~

Subjective side: Change is always subjective. All through evolution you find that the conquest of Nature comes by change in the subject. Apply this to religion and morality, and you will find that the conquest of evil comes by the change in the subjective alone. That is how the Advaitic system gets its whole force, on the subjective side of man.

—Swami Vivekananda

~***~

Success: The four basic factors that I am convinced are involved in successful missions: goal setting, positive thinking, visualising and believing.

—A.P.J. Abdul Kalam

~***~

Success: The success is not in the trophy won but in the race run...

—Swami Chinmayananda

~***~

Success of Love: The success of love is in the loving—it is not in the result of loving. Of course, it is natural in love to want the best for the other person, but whether it turns out that way or not, does not determine the value of what we have done.

—Mother Teresa

~***~

Successful man: A successful man is one who can lay a firm foundation with the bricks that others throw at him.

—Swami Chinmayananda

~***~

Suffering: Suffering is the essence of success.

—A.P.J. Abdul Kalam

~***~

Sufferings: All these sufferings are man-made and it is within man's power to put an end to them.

—*Nisargadatta Maharaj*

~***~

Sun: When the sun sets everything goes to take rest. But as soon as it rises, numerous activities take place on earth. But the sun is not affected by any such activity, as it merely acts according to its nature, by fixed laws, without any purpose.

—*Ramana Rishi*

~***~

Sun rises again: If you feel down, just consider that Sun sinks every night and rises again in the morning.

—*Swami Vivekananda*

~***~

Superstition and bigotry: Superstition is our great enemy, but bigotry is worse.

—*Swami Vivekananda*

~***~

Supreme: Our supreme duty is to advance towards, freedom—physical, mental and spiritual—and help others to do so.

—*Swami Vivekananda*

~***~

Supreme: That which permeates all, which nothing transcends and which, like the universal space around us, fills everything completely from within and without, that Supreme non-dual Brahman—That thou are.

—*Adi Shankaracharya*

~***~

Surrender: Setting aside all noble deeds, just surrender completely to the will of God. I shall liberate you from all sins. Do not grieve.

—*Bhagavad Gita*

~***~

Surrender: The more organized your life is, the more the false idea comes in your mind that you are in control. That doesn't mean you shouldn't take care of things, take care of everything, organize, but know that you are not in control of anything. Then surrender has happened.

—Sri Sri Ravishankar

□

T

Take the blame: Stand up, be bold, and take the blame on your own shoulders. Do not go about throwing mud at others; for all the faults you suffer from, you are the sole and only cause.

—Swami Vivekananda

~***~

Tasting: A Master says, 'This is salt. Books also describe salt. You have read them. Put it in your mouth and see for yourself if it is salty'. What the Master says, you must experience. You can find out only by tasting.

—Ranjit Maharaj

~***~

Teachers: I always bow down to those teachers who are conversant with words, sentences and sources of Knowledge and who, like lamps, have shown clearly to us Brahman, the secret of the *Vedas*.

—Adi Shankaracharya

~***~

Teachers: Oh! Almighty, bless me always to be with great teachers of high thinking.

—A.P.J. Abdul Kalam

~***~

Teachers: The teachers of tomorrow are the students of today.

—Sathya Sai Baba

~***~

Teachings of saints: Nanak, Dadu, Dariya Saheb, Mira Bai, Soor Das, Kabir and Nabbaji have all reached the Mystic Sky and have given out the secrets. Though their teachings are one and the same, their ways of teaching are different.

—Param Sant Tulsi Maharaj

~***~

Team: Team creates environment; environment motivates the team.

—A.P.J. Abdul Kalam

~***~

Tears: They that sow in tears shall reap joy.

—Psalms, 126:5

~***~

Temper and pride: Temper takes you to Trouble, Pride keeps you there.

—Swami Chinmayananda

~***~

Temple of joy: Mind at rest is the Temple of Joy. So long as it is gurgling with its desires, passions and attachments in its stormy surface, the signature of joy gets ruffled out.

—Swami Chinmayananda

~***~

Temple: Our temple of worship is there where outward nature and human soul meet in union.

—Rabindranath Tagore

~***~

Temples and churches: Divine incarnations do not come to bring a new or exclusive religion, but to restore the One Religion of God-realization. Jesus wants temples to be established in human souls, first and foremost; then established outwardly in physical places of worship.

—Paramahansa Yogananda

~***~

Test: Test a servant while in the discharge of his duty, a relative in difficulty, a friend in adversity and a wife in misfortune.

—Chanakya

~***~

Test: The acid test by which an activity can be confirmed as holy or sacred is to examine whether it promotes attachment or avoids bondage.

—Sathya Sai Baba

~***~

That is not I: For all the practical purposes of *Yoga*, the man, the working, conscious man, is so much of him as he cannot separate from the matter enclosing him, or with which he is connected. Only that is body which the man is able to put aside and say: 'This is not I, but mine.'

—Annie Besant

~***~

Things: A thing is only completely our own when it is a thing of joy to us.

—Rabindranath Tagore

~***~

Things: Things don't trouble you, but you go in and get troubles. This chair never says, 'I am yours.' You say, 'It is my chair.' So, who is at fault? Not the chair, but yourself. You have nothing to do with it. You should see the world that way.

—Ranjit Maharaj

~***~

Think: Think clearly and deeply, go into the structure of your desires and their ramifications. They are a most important part of your mental and emotional make-up and powerfully affect your actions.

—Nisargadatta Maharaj

~***~

Thinkers: The crowning glory of a nation is its thinkers.

—***A.P.J. Abdul Kalam***

~***~

Thinking: Thinking is progress. Non-thinking is stagnation of the individual, organisation and of the country. Thinking leads to action.

—***A.P.J. Abdul Kalam***

~***~

Thinking: You eat, and after eating, you should not think about eating. Same thing, sex. You have sex finished; afterwards you should not carry sex in the head all the twenty-four hours.

—***Sri Sri Ravishankar***

~***~

Thinking, movement of: Have you ever sat very quietly with closed eyes and watched the movement of your own thinking? Have you watched your mind working? Or rather, has your mind watched itself in operation, just to see what your thoughts are how you respond to a suggestion or react to a new idea? Have you ever done this?

—***Krishnamurthy***

~***~

Thoughts: A man is but the product of his thoughts what he thinks, he becomes.

—***Mahatma Gandhi***

~***~

Thought: Being kind to yourself in thoughts, words and actions is as important as being kind to others.

—***Anonymous***

~***~

Thoughts: It is impossible to know thoughts before they come. You know them as they come. And, if they are stupid, simply smile at them, laugh at them, and they will move away.

—***Sri Sri Ravishankar***

~***~

Thoughts: Since you alone are responsible for your thoughts, only you can change them. You will want to change them when you realize that each thought creates according to its own nature. Remember that the law works at all times and that you are always demonstrating according to the kind of thoughts you habitually entertain. Therefore, start now to think only those thoughts that will bring you health and happiness.

Thoughts, words, deeds: Your thoughts, words and deeds will shape others and theirs will shape you. Have constructive thoughts, consoling words, compassionate acts.

—***Sathya Sai Baba***

—***Paramahansa Yogananda***

~***~

Throw off: Learn to feel yourself in other bodies, to know that we all are one. Throw all other nonsense to the winds. Spit out your actions, good or bad, and never think of them again. What is done is done. Throw off superstition.

—***Swami Vivekananda***

~***~

Time: The time is always right to do what is right.

—***A.P.J. Abdul Kalam***

~***~

Tolerance: Truth cannot afford to be tolerant where it faces positive evil.

—***Rabindranath Tagore***

~***~

Traditions: Cast away your clothes of traditions that you have inherited, for often those can restrain you from growing in the Love of God.

—***Sant Tukaram***

~***~

Transformation: Transformation is an outcome of a far-sighted vision, innovative mind and guiding spirit.

—***A.P.J. Abdul Kalam***

~***~

Treasure: Whatever we treasure for ourselves separates us from others; our possessions are our limitations.

—Rabindranath Tagore

~***~

True devotee: The most distinguished qualities of a true devotee of Allah are that he keeps his secret concealed, his self safe from sins and performs his duties towards Allah with full responsibility.

—Hazrat Royambin Mohammad

~***~

True modernism: True modernism is freedom of mind, not slavery of taste. It is independence of thought and action, not tutelage under European schoolmasters. It is science but not its wrong application to life.

—Rabindranath Tagore

~***~

True surrender: A true surrender includes both the body and the mind, i.e. a total surrender; body and heart function together. Then only surrender becomes complete. Sant Kabir says, 'Nothing remains to surrender thereafter'.

—Sant Kabir

~***~

Truth: And you will know the truth, and the truth will make you free.

—John

~***~

Truth: The center focus of our life is spiritual growth, is peace, then all other things will be around that. Your first and foremost commitment in life is to be with the Truth, to evolve in Truth.

—Sri Sri Ravishankar

~***~

Truth: Trust is the first step to love.

—Munshi Premchand

~***~

Truth: Truth can be taught up to a point. It has to be assimilated by a person's effort, by self-discipline.

—Dr. S. Radhakrishnan

~***~

Truth: Truth cannot afford to be tolerant where it faces positive evil.

—Rabindranath Tagore

~***~

Truth: Truth has no fear; Untruth shivers at every shadow.

—Sathya Sai Baba

~***~

Truth: Truth is meant for the blessing and upliftment of the entire human race. As the Christ Consciousness is universal, so does Jesus Christ belong to all....

—Paramahansa Yogananda

~***~

Truth: Truth is One. I have often said that if Jesus, Krishna, Buddha, and other true emissaries of God came together, they would not quarrel, but would drink from the same one cup of God-communion.

—Paramahansa Yogananda

~***~

Truth: Truth is simple and open to all. Why do you complicate? Truth is loving and lovable. It includes all, accepts all, purifies all.

—Nisargadatta Maharaj

~***~

Truth: Truth is the perfect comprehension of the universal mind. Beauty is in the ideal of perfect harmony which is in the universal being. We individuals approach it through our own mistakes and blunders, through our accumulated experience, through our illumined consciousness—how, otherwise, can we know truth?

—Rabindranath Tagore

~✻✻✻~

Truth: Truth is your birthright. Assert it and be master of universe. Truth is *Tat Tva Masi* - 'That Thou Art'.

—Swami Ram Tirath

~✻✻✻~

Truth: Whenever our life is stirred by truth, it expresses energy and comes to be filled, as it were, with a creative ardour. This consciousness of the creative urge is evidence of the force of truth on our mind.

—Rabindranath Tagore

~✻✻✻~

Truth: The earth is supported by the power of truth; it is the power of truth that makes the sun shine and winds blow; indeed all things rest upon truth.

—Chanakya

~✻✻✻~

Truth and untruth: All persons should always be ready to accept the truth and renounce the untruth.

—Swami Dayananda Saraswati

~✻✻✻~

Truth in religions: All religions have some truth in them, but none has the whole truth; all are created in time and finally decline and perish. You cannot shut up God in the limitations of your own narrow brain or dictate to the Divine Power and Consciousness how or where or through whom it shall manifest; you cannot put up your puny barriers against the divine Omnipotence. These again are simple truths, which are now being recognized all over the world; only the childish in mind or those who vegetate in some formula of the past deny them.

—Aurobindo Ghosh

~✻✻✻~

Truth is truth: Even if you are a minority of one, the truth is the truth.

—Mahatma Gandhi

~***~

Truth, transmigration: When youth has gone, what play of desire is there? When water has evaporated, what pond is there? When wealth has decreased, what circle is there? When the Truth is known, what transmigration is there?

—Adi Shankaracharya

~***~

Truths: We hold these truths to be self-evident: that all men are created equal; that they are endowed by their Creator with certain unalienable rights; that among these are life, liberty, and the pursuit of happiness.

—Thomas Jefferson

~***~

Truthfulness: When you speak, speak the truth; perform when you promise; discharge your trust. Withhold your hands from striking and from taking that is unlawful and bad.

—A.P.J. Abdul Kalam

~***~

Tyranny, political or social: Political tyranny is nothing compared to the social tyranny and a reformer, who defies society is a more courageous man than a politician, who defies Government.

—B.R. Ambedkar

❑

U

Unarmed: I believe that a man is the strongest soldier for daring to die unarmed.

—Mahatma Gandhi

~***~

Universal assent: Every formula of every religion has in this age of reason, to submit to the acid test of reason and universal assent.

—Mahatma Gandhi

~***~

Understanding: Anger and intolerance are the enemies of correct understanding.

—Mahatma Gandhi

~***~

Unjust law: An unjust law is itself a species of violence. Arrest for its breach is more so.

—Mahatma Gandhi

~***~

Unjust: A weak man is just by accident. A strong but non-violent man is unjust by accident.

—Mahatma Gandhi

~***~

Understanding: To understand anything is to find in it

something which is our own.

—Swami Chinmayananda

~***~

Undertaking: Whenever you undertake to do something, do it thoroughly or not at all.

—Shirdi Sai Baba

~***~

Unity, purity: Unity is divinity; purity is enlightenment.

—Sathya Sai Baba

~***~

Uneducated: The life of an uneducated man is as useless as the tail of a dog, which neither covers its end, nor protects it from the bite of the insects.

—Chanakya

~***~

Unity: The significance which is in unity is an eternal wonder.

—Rabindranath Tagore

~***~

Universal suffering: Greed for wealth and other things, the desire to remain in the company of women, great weakness for tasty foods, ego, a liking for evil company, attachment for relatives; a person, who possesses these six faults, will never experience happiness in life or after death.

—Swaminarayan

~***~

Universe: Look at the sky. We are not alone. The whole universe is friendly to us and conspires only to give the best to those who dream and work.

—A.P.J. Abdul Kalam

~***~

Universe: The universe is but a long dream. The ego sense and also the fancy that there are others, are as real as dream-objects.

—Yoga Vashisht

~***~

Unaware: Often your enemies are created not by your action as much as by your tongue, by your words—how you speak, what you speak, what you do. You do this unaware, completely unaware.

—Sri Sri Ravishankar

~***~

Unknowable: Brahman is known to one who thinks it is unknowable and not known to one who thinks he knows.

—Svetasvatara Upanishad

~***~

Unrighteous retaliation: Though unjustly aggrieved, it is best to suffer the suffering and refrain from unrighteous retaliation.

—Thirukkural

~***~

Unlimited in variety: Indian religion has always felt that since the minds, the temperaments and the intellectual affinities of men are unlimited in their variety, a perfect liberty of thought and of worship must be allowed to the individual in his approach to the Infinite.

—Aurobindo Ghosh

~***~

Unnatural work: Unnatural work produces too much stress.

—Bhagavad Gita

~***~

Unproductive confusion: Plan out your work. Then work out your plan. The former without the latter is a sheer waste. The latter without the former is mere unproductive confusion.

—Swami Chinmayananda

~***~

Unsettle: The wise should not unsettle the mind of the

ignorant, who is attached to the fruits of work.

—Bhagavad Gita

~***~

Use: One whose knowledge is confined to book and whose wealth is in the possession of others, can use neither his knowledge nor wealth when the need for them arises.

—Chanakya

~***~

Useful: Beauty has no utility, because beauty is not a 'means', it is an end in itself. All that is useful in life is only a means. All that is useless, is an end in itself. Do you see that? What is the use of being in love?

—Sri Sri Ravishankar

❑

V

Vain attempts: The tragedy of human life consists in our vain attempts to stretch the limits of things which can never become unlimited, to reach the infinite by absurdly adding to the rungs of the ladder of the finite.

—Rabindranath Tagore

~***~

Valour: Fear of death makes us devoid both of valour and religion. For want of valour is want of religious faith.

—Mahatma Gandhi

~***~

Value: If one has a good disposition, what other virtue is needed? If a man has fame, what is the value of other ornamentation?

—Chanakya

~***~

Vedas: The Vedas are the books of all TRUE knowledge. It is the paramount duty of all Aryas to read them, to teach them to others, to listen to them and to recite them to others.

—Swami Dayananda Saraswati

~***~

Vedic hymn: Vedic rhyme is a poetic testament of a people's collective reaction to the wonder and awe of existence.

—Rabindranath Tagore

~***~

Veil of ignorance: You should try to arrive at the understanding that everything originates from Him. Whatever power, whatever skill you possess—why, even you yourself—from where does everything arise? And does it not all have for purpose the finding of Him, the destroying of the veil of ignorance?

—Sri Anandamai Ma

~***~

Vices: Outwardly, he washes with water, but deep within, his heart is tarnished by all sorts of vices. So how can he become pure? His method of purification is like that of an elephant, covering himself with dust right after his bath!

—Sant Ravidas

~***~

Vidya, Avidya: Pandavas and Kauravas is actually the race between *Vidya* (knowledge, perception) and *Avidya* (ignorance, blurred perception).

—Abhinav Gupta

~***~

Vigilant: Vigilant among the heedless, awake among the sleepy, the wise one forges ahead even as a charger outdistances a weak horse. Vigilance is always praised, heedlessness ever deprecated.

—Dhammapada

~***~

Vigilant and alert living: Alert and vigilant living itself is a *Sadhana* in the true sense.

—Swami Chinmayananda

~***~

Villages: There is an abundance of unorthodox, earthly wisdom in our villages. There are hidden treasures of knowledge in our environment, in the oceans, bio-reserves and deserts, in the plants and animal life.

—A.P.J. Abdul Kalam

~***~

Violation: There is no evil the man will not do, who violates the good law, who speaks falsely, who scoffs at the existence of another world.

—Dhammapada

~***~

Violent, being: When you call yourself an Indian or a Muslim or a Christian or an European, or anything else, you are being violent. Do you see why it is violent? Because you are separating yourself from the rest of mankind. When you separate yourself by belief, by nationality, by tradition, it breeds violence. So, a man, who is seeking to understand violence, does not belong to any country, to any religion, to any political party or partial system; he is concerned with the total understanding of mankind.

—Jiddu Krishnamurti

~***~

Virtuous man: A virtuous man alone can use the instrument of conscience.

—A.P.J. Abdul Kalam

~***~

Visionary: Mistakes can delay or prevent the proper achievement of the objectives of individuals and organisations, but a visionary can use errors as opportunities to promote innovation and the development of new ideas.

—A.P.J. Abdul Kalam

~***~

Vivekananda: 'That man a heathen,' said one man coining out of the great Hall in Chicago, 'and we send missionaries to his land. It would be more fitting that they send missionaries to us.'

—As quoted by Annie Besant

~***~

Vow: A vow is a purely religious act, which cannot be taken in a fit of passion. It can be taken only with a mind purified and composed and with God as witness.

—***Mahatma Gandhi***

~***~

Virtues: Good motives, sincerity and infinite love can conquer the world. One single soul possessed of these virtues can destroy the dark designs of millions of hypocrites and brutes.

—***Swami Vivekananda***

❑

W

Wakefulness: The more you are loaded with desires, the more poor you are, the more weak you are. Strength is wakefulness, and in wakefulness, there is no desire. Remember this.

—Sri Sri Ravishankar

~***~

Waking and dream states: What is called deep sleep, darkness or ignorance is the seed of the waking and dream states. It gets perfectly burnt by the fire of Self-knowledge, and it no more produces effects, like a burnt seed that does not germinate.

—Adi Shankaracharya

~***~

Walk: Walk ye in such wise way that this fleeting world will change into a splend or and this heap of dust become a palace of delights.

—Abdu'l-Baha

~***~

Wall: There is a wall of separation between oneself and others and between you and me. Destroy this wall!

—Shirdi Sai Baba

~***~

Watching mind: Let a wise man watch his thinking. The

mind moves with extreme subtlety and is not noticed. It seizes whatever it desires. To watch the mind is conducive to happiness.

—Dhammapada

~***~

Water and lotus leaf: The water on the lotus leaf is very unsteady, likewise life is extremely fickle. Know that the whole world is devoured by disease and infatuation, and assailed by sorrow.

—Adi Shankaracharya

~***~

Want: Success is getting what you want. Happiness is wanting what you get.

—Dale Carnegie

~***~

Water: In a tank, the water may be so clear that it appears non-existent. Though one who looks into the tank may not see it, yet it is there.

—Sant Gyaneshwar

~***~

Way of life: We have not invaded anyone. We have not conquered anyone. We have not grabbed their land, their culture, their history and tried to enforce our way of life on them.

—A.P.J. Abdul Kalam

~***~

Way of love: If you would walk the way of love, never feel hurt nor yield to anger, but accept pain as a part of life.

—Dada J.P. Vaswani

~***~

We are the church: You and I, we are the Church, no? We have to share with our people. Suffering today is because people are hoarding, not giving, not sharing.

Jesus made it very clear. Whatever you do to the least of my brethren, you do it to me. Give a glass of water, you give it to me. Receive a little child, you receive me....

—Mother Teresa

~***~

Weak: If the citizens of a state are weak, their weakness in turn weakens the rulers, the state itself and eventually causes the entire society to perish.

—Swami Dayananda Saraswati

~***~

Weakness: Anything that brings about spiritual, mental or physical weakness, touch it not with the toes of your feet.

—Swami Vivekananda

~***~

Wealth: Strange! Wealth estranges us all. It is all very strange, the money psychology! When you have not got any, you will pant to get some! When you get some, you grow jealous of others who have more, and feel conceited among those who have less!

—Swami Chinmayananda

~***~

Wealth: Wealth is really a means to work out *dharma*. If one uses it merely for personal enjoyment, it is vainly spent.

—Shirdi Sai Baba

~***~

Wellness: A man's wellness depends upon his degree of contentment.

—Sathya Sai Baba

~***~

Well-trained intellect: One gradually attains tranquillity of mind by keeping the mind fully absorbed in the Self by means of a well-trained intellect, and thinking of nothing else.

—Bhagavad Gita

~***~

Well-wisher: Always celebrate the success of your colleagues and friends.

—A.P.J. Abdul Kalam

~***~

What Gita advocates?: The Gita certainly does not advocate war; what it advocates is the active and selfless defence of *dharma*. If sincerely followed, its teaching could have altered the course of human history.

—Aurobindo Ghosh

~***~

Whole, part: You must understand the whole of life, not just one little part of it. That is why you must read, that is why you must look at the skies, that is why you must sing and dance, and write poems, and suffer, and understand, for all that is life.

—J. Krishnamurthy

~***~

Wholeheartedness: The one excellent thing that can be learned from a lion is that whatever a man intends doing, should be done by him with a whole-hearted and strenuous effort.

—Chanakya

~***~

Why liberty?: What are we having this liberty for? We are having this liberty in order to reform our social system, which is full of inequality, discrimination and other things, which conflict with our fundamental rights.

—B.R. Ambedkar

~***~

Why to me: There is nothing, at any time, in any circumstance, to worry over why this to me?

—Swami Chinmayananda

~***~

Wicked man: There is poison in the fang of a serpent, in the mouth of the fly and in the sting of a scorpion. But the wicked man is saturated with it.

—Chanakya

~***~

Widen your heart: Widen your shriveled heart, make the interests of others your own and serve them as much as you can by sympathy, kindness and presents and so forth. So long as one enjoys the things of this world and has needs and wants, it is necessary to minister to the needs of one's fellow men also.

—Anandamayi Ma

~***~

Wife: A good wife is one who serves her husband in the morning like a mother does, loves him in the day like a sister does and pleases him like a prostitute in the night.

—Chanakya

~***~

Willpower: I learnt from failures and hardened myself with courage to face them.

—A.P.J. Abdul Kalam

~***~

Wisdom: Wisdom fills not the unsteady mind of the man of ruffled serenity; he is ignorant of the true teaching.

—Dhammapada

~***~

Wise: The testimony of the Lord is sure making wise the simple.

—Psalms, 19:7

~***~

Wise: The wise sees knowledge and action as one; they see truly.

—Bhagavad Gita

~***~

Wise man: The wise man should restrain his senses like the crane and accomplish his purpose with due knowledge of his place, time and ability.

—Chanakya

~***~

Wounds: Time, patience and Nature are the best physicians to remove all kinds of pains and heal all kinds of wounds.

—A.P.J. Abdul Kalam

~***~

Wisely and steadily: Substitute wisely, grow steadily and be free.

—Swami Chinmayananda

~***~

Within: Everyone who wills can hear the inner voice. It is within everyone.

—Mahatma Gandhi

~***~

We: Nature, body, mind go to death, not we. We neither go nor come. The man Vivekananda is in nature, is born and dies; but the Self, we see as Vivekananda, is never born and never dies. It is the eternal and unchangeable Reality.

—Swami Vivekananda

~***~

Without fragrance: Work without faith and prayer is like an artificial flower without fragrance.

—Swami Chinmayananda

~***~

Without religion: It is said a man without religion is a horse without a bridle.

—Dr. S. Radhakrishnan

~***~

Women, despicable: For centuries, the leaders of Christian thought spoke of women as a necessary evil, and the greatest saints of the Church are those who despise women the most.

—Annie Besant

~***~

Women's progress: I measure the progress of a community by the degree of progress, which women have achieved.

—B.R. Ambedkar

~***~

Wonder: The significance which is in unity is an eternal wonder.

—Rabindranath Tagore

~***~

Words: Harsh words cannot pierce your body. If anybody speaks ill of you, just continue on unperturbed.

—Shirdi Sai Baba

~***~

Words: One should not hurt others even by words. One must not speak even an unpleasant truth unnecessarily. By indulging in rude words, one's nature becomes rude. One's sensibility is lost if one has no control over one's speech.

—Sarada Devi

~***~

Words of power: Out of purity and silence come the words of power.

—Swami Chinmayananda

~***~

Words, fair: Like a flower full of colour but without fragrance are the fair words which bear no fruit in action.

—Dhammapada

~***~

Worldly state: As long as there is mental preoccupation with causality, so long does the worldly state continue. When engrossment with causality is exhausted, one does not attain the worldly state.

—Katha Upanishad

~***~

Work: Learn to attach your mind completely to your work while you are doing it, and you will find joy in it. But then, don't remain attached; learn to detach your mind from your work at a moment's notice. But this detachment is not indifference.

—Swami Prabhavananda

~***~

Work: Before you start some work, always ask yourself three questions—why am I doing it, what the result might be and will I be successful. Only when you think deeply and find satisfactory answers to these questions, go ahead.

—Chanakya

~***~

Work: Good work is appreciated everywhere.

—A.P.J. Abdul Kalam

~***~

Work: How you all will change the work after I am gone! If I came back a hundred years from now, I just wonder if I would even recognize it.

—Paramahansa Yogananda

~***~

Work and success: Success comes before work...only in the dictionary.

—Dr. S. Radhakrishnan

~***~

World: What's the world like? A flock of sheep. One falls in the ditch, the rest jump in.

—Sant Kabir

~***~

World peace, inner peace: We can never obtain peace in the world if we neglect the inner world and don't make peace with ourselves. World peace must develop out of inner peace.

—Dalai Lama

~***~

Worldly things: By constantly thinking of worldly things, a man becomes calculating and deceitful. He becomes guileless by thinking of God. What will a pundit's scholarship profit him, if he does not think of God and has no discrimination and renunciation?

—Ramakrishna Paramahansa

~***~

Worshipping the lingam: A devotee, who worships the *lingam* or the *yoni*, is thinking of the fatherhood or motherhood of the universe, the source of creation, preservation and dissolution.

—Swami Prabhavananda

~***~

Worthless: Worthless are those who injure others vengefully, while those who stoically endure are like stored gold.

—Thirukkural

~***~

Worthy: Give your wealth only to the worthy and never to others. The water of the sea received by the clouds is always sweet.

—Chanakya

~***~

Wounds and healing: When I stand before thee at the day's end, thou shalt see my scars and know that I had my wounds and also my healing.

—Rabindranath Tagore

~***~

Writing with black ink: To give without sympathy is to build a temple without the idol and is as futile as painting a picture with black ink on a black-board.

—Swami Chinmayananda

~***~

Wrong and right: Let craft, ambition, spite be quenched in reason's right, till weakness turns to might, till what is dark 'be light till what is wrong' be right.

—A.P.J. Abdul Kalam

❑

Y

Yoga not impossible: The Self in you is the same as the Self Universal. Whatever powers are manifested throughout the world, those powers exist in germ, in latency, in you.... If you realize the unity of the Self amid the diversities of the Not-Self, then *Yoga* will not seem an impossible thing to you.

—***Annie Besant*, Introduction to Yoga**

~***~

Yoga: A person is said to have achieved *yoga*, the union with the Self, when the perfectly disciplined mind gets freedom from all desires, and becomes absorbed in the Self alone.

—***Bhagavad Gita***

~***~

Yoga: The meaning of our self is not to be found in its separateness from God and others, but in the ceaseless realisation of *yoga*, of union.

—***Rabindranath Tagore***

~***~

Yoga, for the divine: The *yoga* we practise is not for ourselves alone, but for the Divine; its aim is to work out the will of the Divine in the world, to effect a spiritual transformation and to bring down a divine nature and a divine life into the mental, vital and physical nature and life of humanity. Its object is the liberation and transformation of the human being. It is not personal *Ananda*, but the bringing down of the divine Ananda—Christ's kingdom of heaven, our *Satyayuga*—upon the earth.

—Sri Aurobindo Ghosh

~***~

You and God: On the way to God, the difficulties feel like being ground by a milestone. Like night coming at noon, like lightning through the clouds. But don't worry! What must come, comes. Face everything with love as your mind dissolves in God.

—Lal Ded

~***~

You, the instrument: The power of God is with you at all times; through the activities of mind, senses, breathing, and emotions; and is constantly doing all the work using you as a mere instrument.

—Bhagavad Gita

~***~

You: Because of you, there is a world. To you such statement appears meaningless, but on investigation, its meaninglessness may disappear.

—Nisargadatta Maharaj

~***~

You: Be prepared for the questions that God would ask everyone: 'Could you become you'.

—A.P.J. Abdul Kalam

~***~

You and I: What has God not created for you? Everything is in its proper place. Tuka says, 'When our pride disappears, with it goes the relation of You and I.'

—Sant Tukaram

~***~

"You" and I" thought: When the mirror of my consciousness became clear, I saw that my family and others I love are the same as me. The 'you' and 'I' though do not occur. The entire world is God.

—Lal Ded

~***~

Your children: Treat your kid like a darling for the first five years. For the next five years, scold him. By the time he turns sixteen, treat him like a friend. Your grown up child is your best friend.

—Chanakya

~***~

Your dealings: Your dealings with all should be regulated by love and due justice in accordance with the dictates of *dharma* (righteousness).

—Swami Dayananda Saraswati

~***~

Your own faults: If you want peace, do not see the faults of others. Rather see your own faults. Learn to make the whole world your own. No one is a stranger, my child. The whole world is your own.

—Sarada Devi

~***~

Your ownself: Always bear this in mind: Everything is in God's hands, and you are His tool to be used by Him as He pleases. Try to grasp the significance of 'all is His', and you will immediately feel free from all burdens. What will be the result of your surrender to Him? None will seem alien, all will be your very own Self.

—Sri Anandamayi Ma

~***~

Your secret: The biggest *guru-mantra* is: never share your secrets with anybody. It will destroy you.

—Chanakya

~***~

Your want: All will happen as you want it, provided you really want it.

—Nisargadatta Maharaj

□

Z

Zeal: A policy is a temporary creed, liable to be changed, but while it holds good, it has got to be pursued with apostolic zeal.

—*Mahatma Gandhi*

□□□